MEMORIES

By Joseph DeSanctis

Best wishes

Joseph De Sanctis

12-30-18

ISBN: 0692097708
ISBN-13: 978-0692097700

DEDICATION

I dedicate this simple book to the memory of Reverend Don Gaetano Tantalo, to whom I owe the knowledge of some Latin, but mostly for my interest in music. I met him in the special year I lost my mother: 1935. I was a mess. I avoided all my teenage friends, rebelled at home, and was not a good example to my brother, Luigi, or my sister, Chiara. But Beethoven's and Chopin's lives made me change my disposition.

Don Gaetano offered his life to save the lives of us five men (three young, and two older men) who were condemned to be killed at 9 p.m. on June 7, 1944. I will never forget that day. My stepmother, Concetta Franchi, offered at the altar to Our Lady of Grace in our local church of St. Peter, my one-year-old brother—her son, Domenico—in exchange for my life. I was 20 years old at the time.

TABLE OF CONTENTS

ACKNOWLEDGEMENTS

This memoir has been a work-in-progress for a number of years. I would like to acknowledge my family, who worked together to make it available to my children and grandchildren, and to my family in Italy and the United States:

To my son, Joe, thank you for your transcription of my theme, for obtaining the copyright for my story, and for being my personal Information Technology engineer, driver, photographer and videographer, and "catch-all" support person for Mom and me here in Yonkers. Thank you for your touching foreword, and for embodying and passing on the legacy of faith, music, composing, and performance in our family. Thanks to my daughter-in-law, Lenora, for her love and support all these years, and for her lovely voice. To both of you, thank you for our three grandsons.

To my daughter, Lucy and son-in-law, Pablo, thank you for supporting Mom and me when we lived in

Acknowledgements

Brick, and for our two granddaughters and our grandson. Lucy, thank you for your review of the book, your good opinions and input into the process, and your beautiful foreword. I loved to read about the memories you cherished with our family and I'm proud of the the way you have shared our values with your own family.

To my daughter, Mary, thank you for being the historian for this book, for your hours of "Questions and Answers" to help get the details right, and for your endearing foreword. I loved reading about how your experience in Italy shaped your love of the Italian language, your appreciation of storytelling, and your vocation and leadership as a teacher, musician, vocalist, and supportive wife and mother.

To my son-in-law, Ralph, thank you editing the original manuscript and preserving my voice and my personality in the finished product—a tough job. Thank you, also, for your introduction to the book. I am happy that my story touched you. To you and Mary, thank you for our granddaughter and grandson.

To my niece, Susan, thank you for taking the project to completion and herding all the cats.

To my grandchildren, Christina, Philip, Joey, Marc, Nicky, Angela, Elisa, and Antonio, thank you for the joy you give us all, for your talent and innovation and creativity, and for each of your unique personalities. You are so loved.

Acknowledgements

To my sister-in-law, Frances, my brother-in-law, Tony, and to my relatives who you've met in this story as well as all my family and friends both here in the United States and in Italy—thank you for your love, friendship, care, and for our many meals and stories at the table. You help keep my memories strong.

To my wife, Rose, thank you for your love, support, companionship, and our partnership and solidarity in faith. Oh, and of course, thank you for your pizzelles! We have been co-stars in some fun performances, but most importantly we've raised a beautiful family to love God, music, good food, wonderful stories, and each other.

FOREWORD

Lucy Ortiz
Matawan, New Jersey, September, 2017

At a young age, my dad was separated from his mother and was forced to grow up quickly and take on responsibilities he felt compelled to as the first-born of his family. He spent his youth trying to redefine his role as his family dynamics changed and evolved finding music a welcome retreat from his worries, his studies, and his work.

When the Germans occupied Italy during World War II, resources were limited and people feared for their personal safety and the safety of their loved ones. During this time, my father's faith was tested when he was captured as a hostage by the Germans. Whenever my family is having a challenging day (or week or month) trying to keep up with the bills or worrying about another upcoming or unexpected expense or event, I often remind myself that no matter how challenging the situation might be, my parents had it much harder and they managed to survive.

In fact, if I had to find a common denominator throughout my dad's stories I'd have to say it is faith and resiliency. I'd go further and say that my dad's deep faith is what made him resilient and survive/surpass his challenging circumstances.

The stories contained herein are stories I grew up hearing around the family dinner table or during a social or holiday gathering with friends and extended family members. As my siblings and I grew up and had families or our own, we've since heard them recounted by Dad to his grandchildren at our own family gatherings. We've shared some of these stories with our friends who are in awe of the rich history and legacy we have inherited.

Growing up, the impressions left on my dad through his personal experiences colored the fabric of how he raised us and what he taught us both explicitly and implicitly. His experiences solidified several values he sought to pass onto his children: devotion to faith/gratitude, devotion to family, love of music, and respect for women.

Devotion to Faith/Gratitude

Involvement in the Catholic Church was an integral

part of my dad's upbringing. Growing up, Dad was the organist at our parish and so were my two older siblings. Presently, both of them continue to be involved in music ministry to a greater or lesser extent. Through all the challenges and obstacles my dad faced during the hard times in which he lived, he always relied on his faith in God to propel him forward. As a result he made certain his children understood the importance of going to mass regularly and actively participating in our faith.

When faced with certain execution after being held captive by the Germans, he had a life-altering experience in that he was, instead, released owing to the influence of his living guardian angel, Don Gaetano. In my father's eyes, it was a miracle and as a result, considers his life a gift for which he is forever grateful (as are we).

Devotion to Family

My dad took it upon himself to be the man of the house at a young age in the absence of his mother, who was sick and away from her children, and his father, who was busy working hard to support his family. He felt compelled to protect and care for his younger siblings. He did the best he could and when his father re-married, his stepmother acknowledged his efforts in how she treated him.

I remember my dad worked very hard. He had

several jobs and as a musician—had gigs nights and weekends to make ends meet. Still, we had family vacations together and the occasional dinner outings. He took the time out to play a game or two of cards with us and he taught me how to play chess and ride my bike.

Love of Music

My dad played piano and accordion. He taught all three of his kids how to play both. He also gave private lessons at home. We owned a couple different pianos over several years. The one I grew up with was a baby grand. You couldn't live in that house and not play an instrument, or sing, or both! My brother went on to study performance at Catholic University, my sister, music education at Syracuse University.

Although I didn't study music in college, I loved playing the piano. To me, music was an escape to another world. I'm forever grateful to my dad for sharing his love of music with us. The house came alive whenever we had gatherings. He'd pull out the accordion and the next thing you knew, everyone was singing old Italian folk songs out in the backyard at the top of their lungs!

Foreword

Respect for Women

Most Italian households I know are very matriarchal. There's a definite balance of power between the father and the mother and although the father is usually the main breadwinner and commands respect from his family, the mother has just as much authority but is careful to ensure that the children regard their father as the one who has the final say. Our household was no different. We lived with our maternal grandparents and my dad had a special bond with my grandmother. He admired and respected her and she treated him like another son. Mom and Dad got along fairly well although there were a lot of loud debates between them. (OK, yelling—by the way, did I mention this is also fairly common among the Italian households I know?) Still, definitely there was love and respect between them that still exists today.

Dad and I had a ritual every Sunday: after Mass he and I would visit his aunt, Zia Aninna, and his cousins, Aunt Adele and Uncle Herman, for coffee. Zia Aninna was wheelchair-bound and I was about ten or eleven at the time. She would have me go to the kitchen and prepare the espresso, and when it was ready, we would sit and talk. I enjoyed those visits and it became clear to me that she was a very wise and special woman. She was instrumental in helping my Dad through his initial emigration to the US and he never forgot that.

Foreword

In Summary

Dad gave me a copy of these written pages long before I got married and had three children of my own. To be honest, I hadn't read them all the way through until only recently. As I've already mentioned, many of the stories I'd already heard, but there were others unfamiliar to me. I'm grateful for the experiences he's shared with my family because they've molded my own family values and I can only hope they will help to enrich and guide my own kids and values. Thanks, Dad.

* * *

Joe DeSanctis
  Ossining, New York, September, 2017

February 10, 1948.

It was much later in my life that I found out that my father's arrival in the United States happened 10 years prior, to the day, of my own arrival in this world. You see, my father told me this—and he might have told me more than once—but like a normal adolescent son, I probably chose not to listen. But good for us—he kept on telling us his stories.

In fact, he was always telling us stories, and even

though some stories were constants at the dinner table, every once in a while I would learn something new. It was like catching a missed episode of your favorite TV show! That being said, every story was always embellished with interruptions by my mother who always wanted to corroborate the facts, or more than likely, modify the story for a more dramatic effect. In any case, I know she liked hearing them too.

Somehow these stories always presented themselves with the backdrop of family members all present, seated at their "assigned seats" in the basement kitchen, eating dinner. They were like another member of our family; and close relatives, at that! So I think that is why we are so grateful to Dad for writing these down. As I re-read these words, they are like a warm blanket—so comforting—and they take me back to my seat at that table. What's more, how wonderful to be able to hand them now to our children and loved ones.

My father is a wonderful storyteller because I think he has no filter—he tells them not only how he remembers them, but how he felt at the time and how he feels in the story's latest delivery. You feel so close to the man. Being his son, it wasn't easy to be close to my father at times; especially in my rebellious and radical adolescent years. I think my Dad was caught between his way of rearing children and that of the family he lived with, namely my mother and her parents. So the man I got to deal with every day wasn't this warm, creative, adventurous, and feverishly optimistic and humorous creative. I saw only the ultra-serious, rigorous, fully orthodox, heavy disciplinarian. I just never realized he didn't have a whole lot of time to "figure me out" and I'm sure that frustrated him as well. And like him, I find myself in the same pattern with my own children. Amid my newfound craziness, that realization makes me smile. Dad, you were right, and you did great!

But it needs to be said that my father's writing abilities were not limited to words. In fact, I didn't know he had that capability at all until 1995 when he presented us with this manuscript. Yes, I did receive letters of encouragement from time to time in my college and post-college years. They were gems! And he always talked about music with me. That is where I thought my father's creative genius solely lay. And again, I was wrong—he is an amazing author!

I had the greatest opportunity to see my Dad in action, even during my formative and outrageous teen years. I went with him when he played the 12:30 Mass at St. Denis and sat next to him on the organ bench. I accompanied my father as he did "club dates" and watched him connect and improvise over standards with other musicians, seamlessly without rehearsing, and without using words. He even recorded some of his original music on an old reel-to-reel machine that he acquired with the support of my Uncle Tony (the other big audiophile in our family). I think his desire to perform and record transferred to me, to my sisters, and to our own children. His desire to be remembered as a musician was also a part of his essence.

I think it only fair that Dad's musical prowess be present in his book somehow. And so, I thought a transcription of one of his most "famous" compositions would be not only helpful, but necessary to show the depth of his genius. Here is that theme. I did ask him what he entitled the work, and he said "theme", so this is my father's theme as I remember it...

My Father's Theme

* * *

In 1977, Billy Joel's "The Stranger" album came out and the theme of that album bears a striking similarity to the first measure of my Dad's theme. It was so moving to me that in 1980 I chose to compose a prelude piano piece based on this theme. I believe you can hear my father's yearning for his fatherland—pining for the family and friends far away—and his deep faith in God (and God's plan for him) in this sweet melody. I know I can.

For me, my Dad's story can't be understood without my family as the backdrop, his faith and feelings implicated. First you hear his character in the music, and then you recognize his musical story in the opus of his descendants.

I, too, believe that Don Gaetano continues to watch over Dad and our family in a very special way.

Thanks, Dad, for gifting us the story of your life in words and music. God bless you and keep you.

Love,

Joe

* * *

Mary DeSanctis Carmosino
Brooklyn, New York, November, 2017

I am honored to be Dad's first-born. Because of that, there were many things we got to do together: like sitting at the kitchen table mapping out routes to our vacation destinations, or helping him put my sister's doll house together for Santa.

One Christmas, Dad and I were putting up some last-minute decorations. Mom was setting the table for the big family holiday meal. There was banging in the kitchen from the pots and pans my grandmother was using to make the pasta and gravy; she had already made the meatballs and the smells were wafting throughout the house. Holiday music was playing in the background. I turned to Dad and said something about how chaotic everything was. He replied, "If it weren't chaotic, it wouldn't be a holiday." How true. What I didn't realize at the time is that we were creating a setting for storytelling.

There is a story he tells of my birth that is rather revealing. After hearing me cry in the hospital, he was eerily reminded of his father's screams in the hospital following an attack by the Germans some ten years earlier at the end of World War II. Not exactly a pleasant association for sure, but it does show how much my dad was impacted by the events of his childhood: losing his mother at an early age; his friend, the priest, who carried him through that loss, introducing him to music and actually saving his life during the war. The stories told here are front and center to him most of his days. As he approaches his 95th birthday, he is still retelling these stories. (I heard one of them again recently over a bowl of minestrone.)

Both of my siblings have written about what it was like growing up with Dad and their relationships with him. I certainly echo their thoughts and feelings about that time in our lives. But perhaps because I was his first-born, Dad was determined to introduce me as early as possible to the things he valued. At the young age of 6, I went with my parents to Italy for about 5 weeks. It was the first time either of them had been back there since they emigrated to the USA. While I didn't realize it at the time, I got to meet many of those who populated my dad's stories. I wondered why my grandfather, Emilio, limped. I wondered why my uncle, Zio Domenico, was closer to my age than to my dad's. I wondered why my dad's aunt, Zia Teresina, always wore black. And because I was there during my formative years, I believe the foundations for my understanding and speaking Italian so well were laid back then.

Teaching me to play the piano at a very young age was extremely important to Dad; making sure I learned early in my life what he didn't get to do till much later. Dad has always had a passion for music his entire life, but didn't get to realize that passion until his adolescence. I'm sure Dad didn't want that for me. That's why I don't remember learning how to play. It's as much a part of me as knowing how to walk or talk. I have a picture of myself right after my fourth birthday, all dressed up, sitting at the piano, with music in front of me, and my hair in Shirley Temple curls (thanks, Mom).

My faith formation also started very early. My parents made sure I went to Mass every Sunday. I was taught to say my prayers in English as well as Italian. And by the time I was 12, I was already playing the organ in the parish where I grew up. Dad made sure both my brother and I were part of the parish music scene. Around this same time, I remember hearing conversations about possible sainthood for Don Gaetano Tantalo, the priest who saved Dad's life in more ways than one.

And now, still involved in music as a church organist and music director in a parish with English as well as Italian services, I often have to play for funerals. When I tell my husband that I have another funeral to play, he tells me that I know a lot of dead people. Well, I don't know them, really. But often I do get to learn about them through their eulogies. I have found that there are two topics that are usually delivered in a eulogy: the deceased's character and strengths is one, and the second is food. It could be an Italian mother or sister who made the best meatballs, lasagna, or gravy (tomato sauce) for Sunday dinner. Or maybe someone's dad, cousin or brother who loved his after-dinner coffee with Zambuca. I began to reflect on why food is such a common theme in eulogies. Well, where did they learn about these people's character or strengths? Or hear their stories? Where did we hear Dad's stories? Around the dinner table! Eating food together becomes the venue for sharing recipes, advice, and of course, stories, both of the present and the past.

I love quotes. They always seem to say the things I want to express, but so much better. I recently came across one by a rather obscure Scottish composer and music critic that I think describes the circumstances and events in Dad's life that he relates in his stories in a musical way:

When the pattern of one's life is broken up, everything disintegrates; one's homophony becomes polyphony, one's harmony becomes counterpoint—all becomes chaotic [sic]. Then gradually it settles down, a few dominant themes emerge, then two, then one. And then one begins again. And again the same thing happens. And so on. Until the end.

- Cecil Gray (1895-1951), Notebooks, Pauline Gray (ed.) 1989

And so on, indeed. But, end? Maybe not. Maybe the life lesson here is to continue to gather. To tell Dad's stories. To tell our own.

Gotta go pick up Mom and Dad for the holidays. Mom is bringing her pizzelles for dessert. Dad may want to make his gnocchi for the first course. Who's coming for Christmas dinner?

INTRODUCTION

I don't like memoirs. Let me say that right up front.

Every time I start reading one, my mind immediately begins to flood with questions: Why are other people's lives more interesting than mine? Why do all these intriguing (and sometimes damaging) events happen to them and not to me? Why doesn't *my* life have spectacular themes and fabulous plot lines? And, curiously, why does Amazon keep adding these books to my "Recommended for You" list?

Whenever I try to plow through a memoir, my mind inevitably becomes hostage to those impossible thoughts, keeping me awake in the dead center of the night. I angrily watch the clock—interminably it seems —until the glowing numbers finally indicate that only one single solitary minute has passed. Morning will never come! And neither will the end of the book, I'm afraid.

Like I said, I don't like memoirs. That is, until Joe's

adventures smacked into my life like a meteor crashing into Earth.

I didn't grow up at his family's dinner table listening to his stories being told over and over. I didn't get a chance to ask him questions about how he felt at the time, nor find out who taught him to play music so beautifully. How I wish that weren't so now.

No, I came into Joe's life later, through marriage, getting to know him very much after the events in his story took place. I've always wanted to understand how he nurtured his passion for music, faith, family, and homemade bread (not necessarily in that order). As a young boy, how did he cope with his mother's illness? What was it like living through the German occupation in Italy? And more importantly, why does he love roasted potatoes so much?

When the idea of publishing his story surfaced in one of the many family gatherings, I decided it was time to push aside my trepidations and prejudices and read the manuscript. My own father was starting to lose his memory to Alzheimer's; his history fading like powdery chalk with nothing left but the ghost of a few words on a lone blackboard. I didn't want that to happen to Joe and his story—this was an opportunity not to be missed. So I dove in, pretending to be a teenager at his dinner table years ago, hungry for food but also for words. I am, after all, a reader.

Like any great piece of writing, the story pulled me in

like a temptress. As she turned page after page for me, I was there next to Joe, watching him and feeling his every emotion: crying, laughing, full of innocence. This was not just a memoir; it was a life lesson.

Joe's tragic and comical story is a moment in time, but reverberates for all of us today. It reinforces Love, Comedy, Faith, and Passion in our humanity. The setting is a small village in Italy, but the place is universal. Let yourself fall prey to the temptress. Let her overtake you and guide you; you won't be disappointed.

And now, I'm going to check my Amazon list for another memoir to savor!

With love,
Ralph Carmosino
Brooklyn, New York, November, 2017

PRELUDE

I am getting on in my years and today (a beautiful spring day) is one of the best during my retirement time. I am sitting in the living room on my favorite lounge chair thinking about the options my present position offers, including a little nap here and there.

On my left there is a large bay window that provides plenty of daylight for me to either read or write. I also enjoy the sun's rays on a clear day and the sight of occasional cars, pedestrians, and, without fail, my postman. Directly in front of me there is a large sound system with a comfortable TV set that I can operate with a remote control. Right next to it is a table with a European lamp, a video tape stand, and a sofa positioned horizontally, followed by a dining table with six chairs and a china closet against the wall that completes the living and dining rooms combo. Of course, there are plenty of family pictures and a variety of paintings around the walls.

Over to my right I can see the back end of my house with a big sliding glass door leading to the patio. I also see my spouse Rose and my mother-in-law Maria. They both are in the den, sitting on the sofa with their heads bowed over a puzzle they are trying to finish before Mother's Day. It is a three-thousand-piece puzzle and is larger than the coffee table top that holds it. (I found an appropriate piece of plywood to fix that problem.) Just before that room I can see the doorway to the kitchen on the left, and the hallway leading to the two bedrooms and bathrooms on the right.

Coming back with my eyes, I see my good pastime companion, an English grandfather clock, standing before the door to the utility room and the garage. Further to my right, there is a baby bureau with some books on the top of it and my simple desk with a computer and a printer. Next, I see the foyer with a closet on one side and the front door on the other. Behind my right shoulder there is another table with a lamp that gives me plenty of light to read books, or read music if I desire to play the accordion at night.

In the mornings, sometimes I play the piano in the den. That room also has a fireplace, a smaller entertainment unit with another TV set, and a lounge chair. That side of the house is very quiet in the early part of the day.

I recently picked up the Reader's Digest Encyclopedic Dictionary and looked up the word "faith". FAITH, n.

Confidence; Trust. So, I decided to find out how much this beautiful word has helped my existence so far and how I applied it to my survival kit; in other words, how I put it to use.

I close my eyes and my mind goes back as far as my young age of about seven. Here is my old house where I was born. Here is a big kitchen in which many people move about it. My grandmother Maria is busy with domestic work. My grandfather Domenico is getting ready for his many daily chores. As a part time farmer, he takes care of a little female donkey, a medium size pig, and a young goat; he keeps them all in a little barn not too far from the house. He spends most of his time as a custodian of two churches: St. Peter, our parish, and St. Anthony, a Confraternity.

My father Emilio walks in for lunch after his first half day delivering mail as the only letter carrier in my town, Tagliacozzo, Italy, which has about eight thousand inhabitants. My mother Maria is helping my grandmother and at the same time is supervising her four children: myself, my four-year-old brother Luigi, my sister Chiara, who is a little over one year old, and my little brother, Raffaele, just a few months old.

What a beautiful picture! To my amusement, sometimes the goat is allowed to roam around the house. But what impresses me most is my mother reading to me classical books like *I Promessi Sposi*, by A. Manzoni, or *Il Cuore*, by E. De Amicis. I felt exuberant! I could not ask for anything better at this point. These are the last and only happy moments I remember of my young age.

PART ONE

MY FAMILY. TAGLIACOZZO, ITALY

CHAPTER ONE

My Mother, Maria DiGiuseppe DeSanctis

Only God knows how much I would praise the most beautiful and emotional relationship that ever existed on the face of the earth: mother and son! The immense joy the mother feels, seeing her son growing up before her own eyes and staring at the happy smile that bursts from those chubby cheeks. The first steps, the constant falls, the first words; all small gems grouped together in a splendid crown of happiness, all original.

It's an extraordinary fusion between two human beings that hold the same inseparable identity. The child smiles when mom smiles and cries when mom is sad—but not for long because she is right there with him all the time. Everything seems so beautiful and simple and impossible.

It seemed an earthly heaven that for me lasted very little; it was substituted by a cruel nightmare that persecuted me for a good part of my teenage years and part of my youth. Quite often I concentrated my mind on anything that could help me find ways to remember my mother's character and most of all, the reasons that contributed to the shortening of her very young life.

She was born in Corvaro (Provence Rieti), on April 1, 1895, and died in a hospital in Rome on June 4, 1935, only forty years old. The town of Corvaro is located at the borderline within the Abruzzo region and only a few miles away from Tagliacozzo, my birthplace.

I was told that in 1920, a priest by the last name of Rampa (brother-in-law of my father's older brother Pietro) was the pastor in charge of the only church in Corvaro. My father, a World War I veteran, was recently back home from a brief visit to the United States. He probably accompanied his brother on one of his visits to the relative priest, met my mother, fell in love, and married her. He was 29 years old and my mother 26. They were a perfect couple.

According to furtive talks grasped here and there from little old charlatan women, a good number of young ladies were already chosen for my father. After all, my father was good-looking and financially settled as a post office carrier. Right after the 1914-1918 conflict, not many jobs were available. Few farmers could hardly even make a living.

My father's marriage caused a general resentment from the neighborhood that never forgave him. According to the evil street talk of fake family friends, my father made a mistake, and sooner or later, somehow, he would have to suffer bitter consequences for it.

Idle gossip never had any value, but when they hide a somewhat disguised truth, then they become a serious matter that could cause enough damage to a well-established family like ours. Consequently, an innocent victim like my mother would lose her young life.

I found out later about this all-too-awful situation by reading some letters my mother had sent to my father from the hospital. My father never knew I found those letters in his bedside table. Senseless, rapacious wolves, disguised as pious women who went to Mass and received communion every day, conspired against my mother, all alone in a strange environment, without a single friend. They teased, threatened and told her to leave my father for whom they had other women ready to replace her. Poor woman! Poor Mama!

One of my mother's brothers had received a monetary loan from the priest's family and could not meet the restitution date; in that case, all my father's side of family, including my grandparents, put out all their anger against my mother, continuously. If her brother was no good, my mother could not be any better.

In other words: "persona non grata". Just thinking about all this makes me very angry.

If I could only have grown up a little faster I would have assisted and defended that poor woman. I would have guaranteed her my protection as long as she was going to be there always for me, for my brothers, and sister. I could have avoided all those sleepless nights, all those frightening dreams and would never have gotten tired of calling her: "Mama! Mama!"

All my teenage friends had their mothers except me. What a delusion! What a nightmare! When we were playing and it was getting dark, all my friends hurried home to their mothers who were waiting for them. Instead my mother was in Rome, in a hospital. I preferred to stay out, if not for fear of my father's mood or my grandmother's screams.

"Rome," I thought, "is not for my mother. Rome belongs to all those people whose names I had seen in the history book. The place for my mother is here, home! As soon as I will be a little older I will go, all by myself to Rome, find her and take her back with me, here, where I can again hear her voice reading all those beautiful stories." This is how I remember her: sitting by the fireplace; me standing in ecstasy, enjoying the charm in her eyes, my brother Luigi, usually restless, trying to listen with his mouth open, and my sister Chiara, sitting in her small chair between us busy smiling.

My mother had a very sensitive character and never got mad for our many escapades. I remember one day she was resting after taking the bread out of the oven and carrying it down the cellar. A beggar knocked at our door. As I opened the door, my mother, from upstairs, told him we didn't have a thing. "How come?" I said, "We have all that bread down here!" My mother said: "It's not ours." I didn't get a beating for that, even though I embarrassed her.

Going over those hidden letters, I realized the humiliation my mother felt from her in-laws for that evil loan of her brother's. My grandparents put locks all over the house and my mother was treated like a servant or worse. My father never noticed anything unusual because my mother, even though she was continually suffering, remained silent. If she tried to say something, my father, to avoid a complicated scenario would say: "They are not that wrong, you know?" So, unintentionally, my father contributed to my mother's tragic fate.

Every once in awhile I go over those letters and I shiver just thinking about the anguish my mother felt for her children away from her. She said to my father: "Are you sure our children are well? Keep them home always. Don't let them go out in the bad weather!" and so on.

Often she sent us children's magazines she received from a priest visiting the hospital and sometimes they were duplicates. Luigi and I complained and she wrote back: "My dear children, be happy anyhow! I didn't even realize it. I can't read too much. I ask you to forgive me."

In another letter to my father, written on a Monday, she said: "I wrote you last Friday and again Saturday and I anxiously waited for some news today; instead I didn't get any mail and my agitation is endless. If I don't say how much I suffer it is because I go through such pain I am not able to describe and also because I have wounds in my heart that only your words would heal them. Perhaps our children are sick? Maybe you are sick yourself? While going through hard times? Hope to hear good news soon. I hug you and the children. Always yours, Maria."

In this other letter: "If you knew, my dear husband, how much I suffered! I'm sure now that if I didn't take everything too serious I wouldn't be here today. But I have a plan. I want to get better only for you and the children; I love you so much that I think I'm going crazy. I gained some weight but I'm afraid to say it. It looks like a miracle too real to believe it." To me and to my brother Luigi: "My desire to see you again is my constant dream, days and nights. I hope you always pray for me as I do for you! Love one another, respect your grandparents, your uncles and aunts, but above all don't cause any worries to your father. You see the hard times he is going through right now? During the day he doesn't even have time for a simple lunch and in the morning he is up long before sunrise. My dear children, these are sacrifices that should come to everybody's attention, especially yours. Understood? I hug you and bless you more profusely because I'm so far away from you. Your most affectionate mother, Maria."

I found two postcards all worn out. One was for me and says among other things: "Don't you know your mother suffers so much because she is far away from you? I kiss you and bless you a thousand times. Your mother." The other was addressed to my brother Louis. "Why don't you write with your tender hand and make your mother very happy with a simple letter? Do you know that I think of you continually without any rest? A thousand kisses on your tender cheek."

I also found a postcard written by one of my father's cousins, Nina Giorgetti, resident of Rome. The card is dated June 13, 1935, a few days after my mother's death. It says: "Dear Emilio, excuse my delay in answering your letter, as you know I wasn't feeling well and for three days I was bed ridden with high fever. Anyhow, yesterday I was able to go to Maria's. She is located at Rome's Verano cemetery. Here is the address: No 111 Square, 4th line, 4th grave. There is a wooden cross for now and could be substituted with a marble one later. At the office they told me that she was buried on June 7, 1935. When we have time we will be glad to go visit her. Your cousin, Nina."

That's it! It seems like the conclusion of a book full of fantasies, hopes and sweet memories, but all I got was a lump on my throat that stayed there for quite awhile. I was very young but I made myself a promise to go to

Rome as soon as possible and visit my mother's tomb since I couldn't go visit her while she was alive.

After my mother's and my grandfather's deaths my grandmother took care of us, but also dominated us like a dictator. For that reason my idea to go to Rome vanished from my mind for a while. I remember that even the neighbors were intimidated by my grandmother's provocative attitude.

Just before World War II started, my father remarried and the new family, with the addition of my step-sister Maria and my step-brother Domenico, suppressed somehow the memory of my mother, but not for me. During the war I was in my twenties, more mature and responsible to go as I pleased, but there were problems with either the railroad or the highways services, caused by military operations such as frequent air strikes.

In January 1944, my friend Giovacchino Ruggeri and I, recently graduated from the Teacher's College of Avezzano in the same Province, took a chance to go to Rome (about 50 miles away) by bicycle with the intention of a possible admission to any university. I didn't have a bicycle, but my friend Pasquale Stammitti loaned me his. We took with us a few pounds of potatoes as a fee to park our bicycles in the town of Settecamini (a few miles before Rome), at Giovacchino's friend's house.

Giovacchino's father, who worked as a supervisor for the highways, gave us a lift with a truck to Roccacerro (a village about 6000 feet above sea level, a couple of miles within the line of our itinerary). From there we started our trip down the hill early in the morning, with plenty of mixed ice and snow. We skidded dangerously a few times along the way but what we found very annoying was trying to find a quick shelter (usually under any bridge) for protection from possible machine gun fire from dozens of airplanes that very often appeared all of sudden from nowhere. We knew by word of mouth that they would shoot any type of vehicles they spotted on the highway.

It was already dark when we reached Settecamini, and, after we left our bicycles at Giovacchino's friend's house, we proceeded to Rome partly on foot and partly by hitchhiking. We passed Portonaccio (access to Rome city by the Valeria Way) a few minutes after 8 p.m. and luckily we found an open boarding house. We could hear the sound of gun shots nearby. It was curfew time and nobody was allowed to be on the street from 8 p.m. to 8 a.m.

The next day we realized that the circumstances were in direct conflict with our project. There was confusion everywhere; the war created a nightmare in central Italy. Many offices were closed and the few opened ones were inadequate. I didn't even consider trying to go to Verano Cemetery. We went back to pick up our bicycles and by 8 p.m. we reached Roccacerro after the too-long hill of Monte Bove.

We were lucky again. We found my uncle Don Vincenzo's house open. (He was also a DeSanctis, my mother's first cousin and the only pastor in that village). We couldn't enter Tagliacozzo, because of the curfew order carried out rigidly by the German S.S. We stayed at my uncle's for the night and came home the next day, by bicycle of course. We really acted foolishly but we were very young.

Another dear friend, Toto Cervellieri, a photographer and music lover born in Rome and a resident of Tagliacozzo since his childhood, told me that his father was buried in Verano Cemetery. He promised to accompany me to see my mother's grave as soon as it was possible to travel a little more comfortably. Finally, June 10, 1945, we were able to go to Rome by train. We visited his father's grave first and proceeded to the address I had of my mother's grave. My heart was beating so fast and I felt so emotional that Toto (older than me) noticed and tried to calm me down a little.

We found the plot, but to our dismay we saw that the entire area was a mass of fresh dirt, just like the farmers use for sowing. We located the information office and they said that all the bodies of that plot were removed for cremation a couple of days before. Each plot was being cleared exactly 10 years after each burial day and used for the current day's bodies. We ran as fast as we could to the cremation site hoping at least to get hold of some of my mother's ashes. Impossible! From that day on, and for quite a few years, I felt so miserable for not having been able to do much for my poor mother, either while living or after she died! I was only three days late! God forgive me!

On the other end, I thank God for giving me courage and good will in promising myself to truly respect all the mothers I would come across in my lifetime, and treat them just like the mother I missed so much—such as my grandmother, all my aunts, my stepmother, my mother-in-law, the mother of my children and all the mothers of my grandchildren.

CHAPTER TWO

My Grandparents, Innocenzo and Chiara DiGiuseppe

My grandparents on my mother's side both died prematurely. I don't know their death dates and I don't remember meeting them personally. They lived in Corvaro and even though they lived during my childhood, the distance and lack of modern transportation prevented any contact with them and my two uncles (my mother's brothers, Vincenzo and Augusto), who used to send occasional postcards.

I remember my mother telling me about her parents when I was about nine years old; she had a very deep respect for them. She also told me about her younger brother Giuseppe who was a member of the Roman equestrian police department; he became seriously ill during a heavy training period and died right after that. That must have happened before I was born because I and other cousins were named Giuseppe, after him. That tragic accident alone evidently deteriorated my grandparents' health.

After my mother's death, during my teenage years, all means of transportation improved considerably and it became possible after all for me to visit my mother's birthplace often, as a guest of my uncle Vincenzo, my mother's brother. Those visits made me realize what my mother had told me a few years before—that her family's well placed social and economic state contributed to the medium-to-high education of all the members of her household, and was the basis for my grandparents' austerity and severity. All the photographs I saw of them showed somehow an aristocratic finesse. Nevertheless, I wasn't able to find out more about them.

The approach of World War II first, and my emigration to the United States after, interrupted further research. My grandfather Innocenzo definitely had a rather mild character; for that reason, I imagine, they nicknamed him: "Pane Cotto" which more or less means easy hot bread or an individual of easygoing manners. My grandmother Chiara, judging by looking over her pictures, showed a somewhat regal and severe character, which is essential to the education process of any family.

When my mother told me all this, she also spoke to me about another special gifted lady friend of hers, Anna Francesca Carducci, who, not only had been her best teenage friend, but also the maid of honor at her wedding and my godmother at Baptism. At that time, she lived across street from my grandparents' house. Later on I looked for that lady, but I was too late again! After my mother's death I missed that traditional home atmosphere where you absorb the process of events pertaining to people within the family's circle.

I also remember a very tall man who I called "Zio Pietruccio". I was told he came from Milan and stopped by to visit us. He carried my sister Chiara in his big arms and that made me very happy. I was unable to trace him. I was too young to demand all the news that involved me personally and at the same time I missed the direct contact with people who could update me on everything: my mother's brothers. Honestly, I didn't even try because of that monetary incident! Our faith teaches us about compatibility and forgiveness, but to what extent?

If my grandparents could have lived a little longer perhaps my mother would have avoided all those spasms and would have lived longer herself. She could have had a powerful support to counterattack the devilish wishes of all those wolves who surrounded her. My paternal grandparents would have been more cautious toward her and my own father would have been more explicit in defending her for the children's sake at least.

If only I could have been lucky enough to be very close to the human being who gave me life; the world's dearest individual. I could have avoided all the misery, anguish, tears and sometimes moments of despair during my teenage years without her. God knows how I missed her presence, her help, especially at night when I had my worse nightmares. I could have been so happy to have her by my bedside like all my friends, telling me stories about her own childhood, or about the mysteries of the Bible, Easter, Christmas and the wonderful tradition of the Nativity scene. But, no!

I missed what is the best part of everybody's life. Very often I went through moments of uncontrollable rage against all my mother's enemies. They fatally shortened her life and so denied my essential moral and material support! Thank God my fervent Christian faith usually helped me to return to my common sense. After all, Jesus paid with his own life for the injustices and faults of all of us.

It seems strange to associate the memory of my maternal grandparents with that of my mother, but she was the only one who told me about them and strange circumstances prevented me from finding out more. Patience!

Here, now, sitting in my favored chair, I close my eyes again and wonder about the scene in my childhood's home…

Suddenly my mother is missing. I was told that she would be back in a few days. But my young brother

Raffaele was given to a neighborhood woman to be nursed. From then on I became very rebellious, disobedient and mad at everybody. Everyday I was outside of that woman's house demanding my baby brother back. He belonged to me and not to that lady. I felt very depressed and helpless. I remember running to a nearby wooded area and crying for a while until I finally calmed down a little.

One day my father told me that mom would not be able to come home for quite a while; she was in one of Rome's hospitals. In the meantime my brother Raffaele died and with him died my hope of seeing my happy family together again.

Although I was under the good care of my grandparents, I felt desperate and at the same time I feared for my brother Luigi's and my sister Chiara's welfare, since they cried continuously. As a firstborn, I felt somehow responsible for them. In my own way I set up a protection rule for them. In the meantime, I deteriorated physically and mentally; I avoided all my school friends, and my belief in God was vacillating although living in a strong Catholic atmosphere. I felt my life was useless.

Around this time I became interested in music. My grandfather Domenico, almost every Sunday morning used to go and help the monks of the convent of Maria Santissima dell'Oriente, about three miles away. In exchange, one of the friars, Father Eustachio Farina, a professional musician, promised my grandfather he would teach me some music. In the beginning I feared his very deep heavy voice, but little by little I felt more and more comfortable and became increasingly anxious to learn.

The interest in music magically diminished my despair. My hope for a better future returned but only for a brief period of time because a little later my sister Chiara passed away. Now panic took hold of me. Wherever I went, my brother Luigi had to be with me. As a firstborn, I felt I failed to protect my own brother and sister. If anything should ever happen to Luigi, I was determined to go with him. We missed our mother terribly. She sent us cards and children's magazines from the hospital on our name day or birthday and we reluctantly accepted that substitution of her own person. "Why can't she come home yet? Why can't we have our own mother home like all our friends?" I hated everything and everybody!

I felt a little relief when my brother started school. At least I knew he was safe in a classroom. At that time, my music interest made me realize the variety of emotions expressed by musicians of different ethnic backgrounds. Other people suffered what I was suffering and were able to let the world know about it through their music. It was magic! I was not alone.

For the first time I saw my chance of exploring the world around me and believing in the possibility of accepting my position in the hands of an almighty power that guides all human beings. If I could change my anger to trust and confidence in myself and in God, I would be at peace with my relatives and my friends. Just thinking all this made me somehow happy. Chopin, while giving concerts in France, was aware of the destructive war and fire in his homeland, Poland. Although very depressed, he expressed with beautiful music, trust, and confidence in a better future for his family and his country.

But soon more calamities came my way. On June 4, 1935 (I was eleven years old) my mother passed away and on July 19, so did my grandfather Domenico. A ray of light had just entered into my turbulent life but was suddenly replaced by a deep darkness I called terror. Only a diabolical force could create such a tragedy for my family, I thought.

CHAPTER THREE

My Father, Emilio DeSanctis

My father Emilio DeSanctis, was born in Tagliacozzo, province of Aquila, on March 4, 1893. Except for the four year world conflict of 1914-1918 and a couple of years of residence in the United States, he continually lived in that town until his death, on June 12, 1967.

During his youth, he received a few lessons in Solfeggio (basic musical sight singing and theory) with discouraging results; nevertheless he had a special music talent that allowed him to play the organ in church, using perfect chords worthy of expert musicians. What can I say about his voice? During the thirties he was the only organist/cantor in town. Four of the churches were equipped with very old organs; for the other three churches he provided his own portable instrument called the Harmonium, or pump organ. (My brother Luigi continued to use it throughout his life.)

I used to go into ecstasy by looking at him play and hearing him sing. He encouraged me to do the same, and during the Christmas and Easter religious services I sang melodies and he harmonized perfectly. We received continuous compliments not only from the priests but from the people as well. That was my first musical experience which fostered my initial interest in music. From then on I dreamed of taking music seriously as soon as the opportunity was available.

When my mother was still living, my father often showed exuberant moments of happiness by whistling so beautifully that I remember standing by with my mouth open. I also remember he had a special whistle that allowed all of us in the family to establish our whereabouts in case we would get lost in a big crowd—more or less, the precursor of the modern cellular phone.

Before the war of 1914-1918, my father came to the United States for work, and took up residence in Yonkers, NY. He found some work in the construction line. I found out later that on his first day on the job, he traveled by a sort of wagon from which he got out before the complete stop, and naturally lost his balance. His boss yelled, "Are you nuts or something?" My father thought he was giving him fatherly advice and answered, "Yes!", the only word he had learned in a couple days here. For that he was fired before he even started. I imagine he wanted to impress his boss somehow. That misunderstanding was soon clarified, however.

I also found out that sometimes on weekends he played the piano at Baiocco's bar on School Street in Yonkers, enough to earn a little extra money. His job as a construction worker, paid very little and was very dangerous. Once he got minor injuries in a coal mine accident.

When Italy went to war in 1914, my father, and some of his friends and relatives of the same age, volunteered to go back and fight for their country. During his second year on the front line, he was slightly wounded on one hand. He said that the food was very scarce and on more than one occasion they fed themselves with cats, mice or whatever they could find.

In the four war years, at different times and places, he had happy reunions with his two first cousins, Rinaldo and Dominic Antenucci, and with his brother-in-law Quirino Di Giampaolo. Rinaldo died in action sometime before the end of the war.

During the Caporetto retreat (a battle on the Austro-Italian front in 1917), my father passed through the city of Gorizia in North Italy, and in one of the buildings damaged by the war he found a piano and began playing it. He started to play the Italian Royal March. Suddenly a group of officers walked in the room, and one of them touched my father on the shoulder. When my father turned his head and recognized the King of Italy, Vittorio Emanuele III, he stood up petrified. But His Majesty whispered in my father's ear, "Continue, son!"

When the war was over, my father came back to the United States for a year or so. Luckily, he found out that in his hometown of Tagliacozzo there was a vacant post office position for the only mail carrier in town, and it was available to war veterans only. He applied for the job and got it. He kept the job until his retirement in 1957, with the exception of the time he had to spend in the Policlinico Hospital in Rome after the accident on his leg during World War II in 1944.

I remember his medium height and good physical health well-tempered by the four long war years. How otherwise could he endure the moral and physical responsibility for his family since 1928? With my mother Maria, myself, my brother Luigi, my little sister Chiara, my little brother Raffaele, and both my grandparents all under his care.

In spite of his energetic will to provide everything and protect everybody, one calamity after another made him very unhappy. My little sister Chiara died in 1929, my little brother Raffaele died in 1934, and the final blow came in 1935 when both my mother and my grandfather died. I was eleven years old, and continually frightened watching my father always upset for what was happening around us. He often yelled at me and at my brother Luigi for peculiar reasons. Secretly, I not only forgave him, but admired his solid courage.

Besides his job at the post office, my father was also custodian of two churches: St. Peter and St. Anthony the Abbot, both in the Alto la Terra section of town and near our home. This activity involved not only my father, but all the members of the family as well. We were responsible in preparing all the necessary items, not only for the Sunday services, but for every day's Mass, including the hosts, wine, water, cruets, vestments, incense, incense holders, candles, etc. Everything had to be continuously cleaned, including the pavement. We also took care of the bells.

On many occasions, my father not only served the Mass but also played and sang for it. Luigi and I did the best we could to help him, and soon we felt like we were living in church altogether.

One of my jobs was playing those blessed bells every day at sundown (the Angelus, which is the triple ringing of the bells for the recitation of the Ave Maria, or Hail Mary) and then locking the church for the night. I also played the bells in the morning as a reminder to the people about the daily Mass. I played them on Sundays, three consecutive times at intervals of few minutes each. If an important feast took place and involved the whole town, I played the bells at St. Anthony's, while my brother played those of St. Peter's, which were much easier to handle. Seven churches in all played bells at the same time and what a sound! We used to show off our special patterns to the point that people could pick the best bell player in an improvised contest, just like a soccer game.

The church of St. Anthony was not a parish but a Confraternity, managed by a group of men who administered its estate. It was mostly land leased to local farmers. One of the activities of the Confraternity was to provide vestments to young boys who participated in the processions of the most important religious feasts in town. These vestments consisted of a long white tunic with a hood that had two holes in it for the eyes, a black half-length cap and a black cord with a bow on either end, for a belt.

The older, stronger boys had the job of carrying different sizes of heavy banners. After the procession, the Confraternity provided special bread baked with anise grains inside, and wine to celebrate the success of the procession. Naturally my father and all of us in the family were responsible for that detailed program.

The feast of St. Anthony the Abbot falls in the winter, during the month of February. The highlight of that feast is the benediction of all the animals. When I was six years old, in 1929, we had a very bad snowstorm. I remember looking out the little window in the sacristy.

All the men were busy shoveling the snow off the roofs of their homes. So much snow had accumulated in the streets that it was impossible for the people and the animals to get to the church.

My grandfather had a little female donkey, a pig and a young goat. He kept them all in a small stable near the church. Every year we kids had a grand time in tending our animals for the blessing outside the church, after the Mass. We missed that event that year. Only a handful could attend. Too bad!

It was very cold in that church, and as a matter of fact, there was a huge brazier (a reservoir for hot coals used for heating) covering about one third of the sacristy floor, always full of thick ash. To provide enough burning coal for that brazier, my father used an old large iron frying pan to which he attached three steel wires forming a hook at the other end like an upside-down umbrella. He filled it with coal and pieces of a newspaper, then he lighted it with a wood match and swung the whole apparatus back and forth, outside the church.

A few times I did that with shivering teeth in the middle of the winter at four o'clock in the morning, right in front of the church. It was a few minutes that seemed an eternity. We had to do that a few consecutive times to fill up the brazier.

St. Anthony's Confraternity was also responsible for transport of the dead to the church and to the cemetery.

For that purpose, it had two instruments called Cataletti, sort of coffin holders or biers. One for the poor people, the other for the better class. The upper class one was nothing but a massive rectangular wood table attached to four wood legs, one on each corner and four extended poles for transportation purpose. The other basic one had the same rectangular shape with a recessed center made with heavy iron straps, like a giant cage, and that, to my opinion, served the purpose much better than the classy one.

These two pieces of equipment were kept in a windowless room on the right side of the church with the side door locked from the inside. We had to go through the main door of the church first in order to open the access door to the coffins, and then we had to walk back the length of the church in complete frightful darkness. For a while that was my job, and the first few times I panicked just thinking about all the strange stories of phantoms and ghosts going around the neighborhood, or of dead people who were trouble-makers even when they were living.

On the left side of the church, there was a long room of the same length as the church, equipped with wood benches lined up along the outside walls, under huge windows which provided light to the church as well. This room was mostly used for monthly meetings by the members of the Confraternity.

To the right of the altar there was a door, which to the

right, led to the organ and the coffin room, and to the left, led to the opposite side of the church where we went to play the bells (whose ropes hung from two holes in the ceiling). A long, completely dark hallway. Everything in complete darkness! All the religious holidays were spoiled just thinking of going through that door to play those blessed bells.

There was a tiny window close to the ceiling that made things worse because it convinced me that somebody was always behind me ready to attack. It was enough to scare any grownup, so imagine me, a skinny ten-year-old boy! Nevertheless, the circumstances of my father were more serious than my senseless fears.

During Easter time, there was activity in a small church called Calvario (Calvary), on the outskirts of the town. It was managed by the same Confraternity of St. Anthony and naturally under my family's care. Every Friday during Lent, a Mass was celebrated there by the Confraternity's chaplain. We had to provide all the necessary items for the ceremony, including twelve candles in the candelabra high above the altar. The last hermit resident who took care of that little church's maintenance had died a year earlier. He was buried there under the pavement of the church, just like the rest of them.

I will never forget one of those first lent Thursdays, about sunset. The chaplain Don Alfonso Tabacco stopped by our house and said that early the next day he was going to celebrate the first lent Mass in that Calvario church, and please provide everything, including those twelve candles in the candelabra. That little church is detached from the last houses on the far top end of town, and at the end of fourteen stations of cross, along the steep hill walk to the church.

I started to walk with my bundle of candles, altar cloths, etc., toward the end of town, hoping to meet at least one of my friends for company. Nothing to it! It was already dark when I got there. I opened the front door very slowly, with a little apprehension. I kept my eyes focused at the round metal cover in the middle of the church's floor, where many people—including the hermits—were buried. I stepped up to the altar and turned around so I could also keep my eyes at the two side doors: one leading to the sacristy and the other leading to the hermit's residence. A faded moonlight came in through the open front door, right in front of me.

I lit the first candle (which I needed to warm the bases of the other eleven in order to set them in the candelabra) but my eyes were fixed on the two doors and the metal cover, as if expecting something to happen at any moment. I was really shaking while trying to set those candles straight while looking elsewhere at the same time.

I was putting the eleventh candle in place when I heard a strange noise that little-by-little, intensified to the point that the whole church trembled. I kept looking with terror at the two doors, waiting for some kind of devil to emerge. I panicked and tried to jump, but practically fell on the floor. To my horror the door in front of me closed shut.

I remember screaming insanely. I flew out of that church like a wild animal, and in a matter of seconds I found myself at the base of the hill. Right at that moment, a huge oversized truck was coming on the highway around the hill, causing all the noise and the vibrations.

The next day I met the chaplain who complained about the twelfth candle!

Right above St. Anthony's sacristy, there was another floor that many years earlier served as the living quarters for my grandparents Domenico and Maria. According to what my father had told me, all their children were born there: my uncle Pietro, my aunts Adelaide, Teresina, Luisetta, and Annina, and my father himself. It seems that the whole family was involved in the church's affairs. My father, the only one who remained home, inherited the tradition.

During my adolescence, a large family rented that whole house. I knew that in the floor of one of the rooms there were two holes through which ran the ropes for the two bells. As soon as that family found a new apartment, the access to the bells through that apartment's door became for me a delicious pastime; no more that nightmare of darkness. A beautiful little piazza we called Ara was right behind the church, and for us kids was a little heaven. We played all sorts of outdoor games such as Ciccio (a game played with a small piece of wood hit by a larger piece to see how far one can make it fly), Tingolo (a cross between hide-and-seek and tag), Piastrella (a hopscotch type of game, as well as a game where one strikes a wall with a rock and the winner is the person who can have it bounce the furthest away from the wall). What a beautiful time!

Going down the hill from that piazza, there was a door to a large room of the Paoluzi palace (the residence owned by the sole remaining Paoluzi family member who was a well-respected lawyer) that had the main entrance on Via Valeria, on the opposite side. It was used as an elementary school classroom. I spent my first elementary school year there in 1929, with the teacher, Alfredo Santini, whose son later became one of my best friends and a doctor here in the USA. I also remember that another room above that one was used as an improvised hen house, and many times we kids found dust on our desks mixed with little white insects that kept our mothers busy every night with thick combs.

A few more steps down that hill lived Zia Peppa, my grandfather Domenico's sister, with her daughter Graziosa and her husband. That house was a blessed shelter for me and my brother Luigi when things didn't go too well in our own home as far as food was concerned. I'll explain!

Every time Luigi and I saw small pieces of tomato skin in any soup, it was pandemonium. We didn't like it, and if there was no alternative, we ran to Zia Peppa's house unless we decided to skip a meal for the day. We preferred more simple and less healthy cheap food. Foolish!

We were too young to appreciate all the precautions my father took for our well being, such as clothing, food, etc., while experiencing so many inconveniences. Very early every morning he played the organ in the two churches: St. Cosma and Annunciation, both located in the lower part of town, way before the post office opened. As soon as he got to the office he started with the Sfoglio, a sort of a route planning device for different town zones, to avoid going to the same place more than once. That job alone kept him busy at least two hours before the regular distribution. In all it was a very heavy job for one man. Just think that Tagliacozzo at that time had a population of about four thousand people!

I remember a few times (mostly in the summer) I met my father during his work time and saw with incredible apprehension, vapor coming out his jacket where it met the heavy belt of the mail bag which was full of letters and newspapers pressing on it. He was also carrying a package or two in one hand. Most often, compassionate people he met on the way gave him something to drink.

Every summer, vacationers (mostly from Rome) took residence in the suburb, and so created a bigger distribution area for my father. And what about dogs? There were plenty of them, and they were not very friendly. My father quite often had to shop for a new jacket or a new pair of pants. But, thank God, there was no physical damage. "Not too bad," was my father's comment. Today, so many years later, there are three postmen covering the same territory, and using modern means of transportation like cars, motorcycles, etc.

I was aware of this situation and I tried to do all I could to help him by taking care of the church services in the morning and sometimes in the afternoon. I was also able to help him distribute some mail during his lunch time in the upper part of town called Sulla Terra, where we lived. Nevertheless, my haughty grandmother complained to my father about our very insignificant escapades, and so made our home life more difficult.

One day, my friend Alfredo D'Ilario invited me to go with him to look for snails. I didn't know much about them, while he was an expert at it. We went out very early in the morning and walked toward the countryside, carrying two long steel wires which we would use to insert into the snails. After walking almost two hours, I didn't find anything but my friend had found five snails. He was much shorter than I and could easily get under any size rock and crawl into any small hole, and that made me feel very uneasy. A few hours later I came up with some snails of my own, but I was scared stiff at the sight of a snake unraveling under my nose. All in all, I had seven snails while he had more than twenty.

At dusk, we headed home. Very disappointed, I expected at least a word of compassion or encouragement from my grandmother, but instead I faced my father who, without a word, kicked me so hard from behind that I banged my head at the top of the bedroom door frame. I didn't have a chance to run the other way. "How come?" I thought. "This is not right!" Not only did my father not realize my state of depression at that moment, but he treated me like a criminal or something.

It took me a long time to understand all the worries that at the time troubled my father, who was continually in a bad mood. He was recently widowed, and responsible for the welfare of his children, and also had custody of my grandmother who was getting older by the day. So after a rough work day, he came home and didn't find his first born—the one he depended on —and then topped off with my grandmother's complaining, he could not have reacted any other way.

That was the only time my father ever hit me. He was right, and I never forgot that circumstance, not even after I settled in the United States.

Many nights I dreamed of that incident that took the shape of a nightmare. Little by little over the many following years, I built up a strong desire to go back to Italy and visit my old house, now owned by other people, and to verify with my own eyes the height of that door frame. Finally, after thirteen years of living in the U.S., I went back for the first time together with my wife Rose and my six-year-old daughter Mary. I entered that house and stood with my mouth open looking at that door frame. It had caused me so much pain but was no more than a couple of inches taller than me. Naturally it was because I had been so small.

I am glad that visit calmed down my constant anxiety. Come to think of it, I handled my own son Joseph more or less the same way, many years later. I knew my father was right and I forgave him even though it was not necessary; I hope my son did the same with me. We never talked about it.

When I started to play the organ and learned to sing the Latin Mass, I was attending the Magistrale School in Avezzano (the secondary school for the training of primary teachers, attended by students aged 14–18) in our province, about ten or fifteen miles away from home. I traveled by train and had to be at the railroad station by a quarter to seven every morning.

My father made me play the Mass in the church of

Annunziata, near the station, at seven a.m. Before I came out the house at six thirty, my father always had breakfast ready for me and in the winter he roasted and peeled the chestnuts which I put in my pockets so I could feel nice and warm while running down the hill to the church and eating at the same time. A beautiful memory! I know now my father was making huge sacrifices for us all.

My father inherited from my grandfather the art of wall cloth-covering. I'll explain. In the basement of our house we had four large wooden cases filled with sheets of multicolored cloths with bizarre designs and tiny pearls on them. When an important feast came along, my father was commissioned to cover with those sheets the walls around an improvised altar out in the open, or on the facades of a building around the balcony, from which the presiding priest would deliver his sermon to the people assembled in the piazza below.

I think this tradition is associated with the Palio ceremonies which take place annually in some big cities in North Italy: Venice, Florence, Siena, etc. My father continued that special task even after World War II, which left him with a stiff leg. He insisted on going up that long ladder, in spite of our continuous warning. Finally my brother Luigi took that job away from him and he is still at it to this day.

CHAPTER FOUR

My Grandfather, Domenico DeSanctis

My grandfather Domenico was born June 11, 1854 and died July 19, 1935, about one month after my mother. What I remember about him is more than I remember about my mother who had been away in a hospital in Rome for so long. He was of medium height, but physically was well built. He busied himself church affairs besides his chores as a part-time farmer. He was a church custodian at St. Peter's parish where I was born. He wore small round eyeglasses with shining metal rims. He read religious books and very often read Latin, making sure he had the right pronunciation even though I doubted he knew what he was reading about.

I'll never forget the holiday Masses, especially Christmas and Easter, he participated as cantor, standing at the end of the balustrade just before the sacristy door. His voice always added a gratifying tone to the festivities. I used to serve the Mass, and I remember being so happy to witness his excessive seriousness for the occasion, and the importance of his mission compared with that of other men his age. I felt so proud of his firm and sure voice that I thought myself to be different from the rest of the boys my age.

But this beautiful mood could change to a sudden hurricane if something didn't go according to my grandmother's plans. On a few occasions my younger brother Luigi and I found ourselves tied together with a three-inch thick belts that my grandfather took off from his pants. My grandfather always tried to be a mediator between his irascible wife and us two noisy and naughty boys, but I am sure his intentions were meant for me to remember otherwise.

I remember him as being very calm; he hated all wrong-doings and was totally submissive to my grandmother who more or less dominated everybody in the family. He always wore a small white flower in his jacket buttonhole and for that he was nicknamed "Fioretto". The whole household inherited that nickname, and we all were proud of it.

All that charm ended on July 19, 1935. He was eighty years old. I remember it was a Thursday because his daughter Teresina, my aunt who lived in Poggetello, was visiting—just like she did every Thursday. It was, and still is, mercato (or market day) in my town. She usually stayed a couple of hours before walking back the three kilometers to Poggetello. But this particular day my grandfather was sick in bed, and later in the afternoon he got worse, so my aunt decided to stay overnight and sent me back to Poggetello to bring her food to her husband Quirino.

It was summertime and I didn't mind walking that far, but I was scared just thinking of passing in front of the cemetery right before entering that little town. I walked and ran at the same time, hoping to pass that blessed cemetery before dark. It was worthless! When I got a few feet from the cemetery everything around me was a black, deep darkness, I could only make out the closed lock of the main gate.

Slowly I passed, walking sideways, and even took a few steps backwards, keeping my eyes fixed on the gate. Then in a flash, I turned and ran as I had never done before. I was convinced that some evil spirit was out to catch me because I felt some of the little rocks hitting my behind. A few minutes after, I met my uncle waiting in the middle of the street. Panic stricken, I turned around but found nobody. I then realized that while running, my own sneakers had lifted those rocks behind me.

Anyway, instead of words of encouragement from my uncle, I had to listen to his complaints and worries about his wife. I stayed there for the night, and came back home the next day. My grandfather had died sometime before midnight. I felt really bad about it.

CHAPTER FIVE

My Grandmother, Maria Casale DeSanctis

Unfortunately, my grandmother Maria, although very dear to my memory, did not have the same character as her husband. She was a little taller than him, very authoritative, and too often upset about very simple inconveniences, and sometimes her own friends were afraid of her dubious mood.

She was extraordinarily robust and had the solid wrists of an adult man so she was able to carry a heavy water jug not on her head like a normal woman of the time would, but on her chest instead, keeping it firm with both wrists; she walked for at least fifty feet from the fountain to the house plus at least ten steps up to the kitchen in our house in Tagliacozzo, Via Valeria, 23.

She could not write or read, but she was so sure of everything she did or thought, and had a fantastic memory even at the age of ninety. Her memory started to fail a couple of years before her death in 1950 at the age of ninety-five. She commanded everybody on anything, and was always right over everybody on everything; after all, she said that she conceived and raised fourteen children, more or less like an army general conquers fourteen fortresses. Unbelievable! Even today I ask myself, "What would have happened if she knew how to write or read?" Poor us! Poor everybody!

Don Gaetano Tantalo, a holy priest of exceptional knowledge, modesty, and iron will, was the pastor of our church of St. Peter. He perceived the imminent changes in religious activities later adopted by the Second Vatican Council of Pope John XXIV so as to have the whole parish participate (young and old, men and women) in every religious service. All the prayers had to be said aloud and slowly as to understand the meaning of each word, even though Latin was still the official language and most people didn't know the meaning of their prayers.

Father Tantalo, or Don Gaetano as we came to call him, also improved our hymn repertoire. As an expert music connoisseur, he taught us young kids all new songs which little by little were learned by the adults. At this point I like to mention the arrogance of my grandmother who, as usual, had to be ahead of everybody and so anticipated the first tone on each phrase in all the hymns, causing discordant confusion here and there. All that used to make me very uncomfortable, while that poor priest, champion of humility, looked at her in ecstasy.

On one occasion, my brother Luigi disobeyed my grandmother (I don't recall the reason) while she was peeling some potatoes with a very sharp pointed knife. She suddenly turned around and in a flash threw that knife at my brother. I saw the knife's handle hanging from my brother's right buttock; he didn't have time to run away fast enough. He had to be taken to the hospital. My grandmother felt very bad about it and I saw her crying for a change.

She took care of all the cooking for my father, my brother, and myself, while keeping the job as a church custodian inherited from her husband. She went up the bell tower to play the bells and she prepared all the accessories for the Masses, including cleaning the linens. Perhaps old age and her overworked schedule contributed to her mental instability.

Most of her friends were already gone by the time she turned 80, and as an octogenarian, I think she waited her turn by acting hostile. I noticed that every time she was told of the death of any friends her age, she said, "Good for her! God spared her all the suffering of this world." But afterwards, when she was all alone, she cried silently as if somehow she wished to avoid her turn.

When her husband was alive, every day she

complained about pains all over her body and found amusement in sending that poor man, my dear grandfather, all over the house to look for anything that could help to calm her down: warm water, towels, all kind of herbs to boil, semolina, leeches, etc.—as long as it could help to lower those unbearable screams. That was her way to get special attention from all of us.

All those pains disappeared after my grandfather's death. If someone had asked her, "What happened to all those pains?" she would snap back, "My husband took all my pains with him to the cemetery!" She did and said unpredictable things all the time.

Her activities in the kitchen slowed down after my mother's death, when my father remarried. Even though my step-mother, Concetta, was in charge of cooking, my grandmother would not give up telling her what to do. To this day I still ask myself, "How could Zia Concetta bear my grandmother's attitude and strange behavior for so many years?" On the other hand, I believe that the memory of my grandmother's own suffering as a young girl, made her somehow hostile to my stepmother, and treated her as a strange individual who invaded our family life.

Often she said that she was very young when her mother died, and suffered a lot when her father remarried a woman my grandmother called "Pessima" (awful). At the young age of ten, my grandmother had to do all the hard work in the kitchen, and when her stepbrother Luigi was born, she very often had to carry a heavy bundle of clothes and wash them in the Imele River (about a mile away) long before sunrise.

On one of those trips, on a very dark winter morning, she found the road blocked by a dead man's body stretched across the road; she was able to go around it, through private property. She said she was a little bit scared, but just thinking about facing her stepmother with any excuse made her continue on her trip to the river. A few minutes later, she said she came across another corpse who was dead even longer than the first one.

This time she didn't have an alternative, so she crossed over the body and tripped on one of the man's pant legs that tore apart like burnt paper. She reached her destination but was really scared stiff, and for awhile she stood there, terrified. When her stepmother came to pick up the washed clothes, she didn't pay any attention to my grandmother's pleas, instead she gave her a good beating.

Her other duties were baby sitter, nurse, sales girl, etc. I'll explain. My great-grandfather Francesco sold fresh eggs for a Roman market, and the only way to transport them was on foot. For that, my grandmother had to travel often through the mountains to Rio Freddo (at least twenty miles west), carrying a heavy basket full of eggs on her head, and at the same time dragging along her stepbrother with one hand and food in the other.

On one of those trips, the boy had a terrific pain in one of his teeth covered with inflamed gums. My grandmother had no alternative and no time to worry, so she made an incision in the gum with one of those pocket-sized knives that are essential daily tools for any outdoor activities, and continued on calmly as if nothing ever happened. The egg business had priority over the baby's health according to the conditions imposed by her stepmother's dictatorial orders.

A couple of times during these trips, she came across individuals of questionable whereabouts. They had long beards and wore colored shirts, mostly red; they were armed with either rugged rifles or knives of all shapes. The majority of them were looking for either food or water, while others asked for directions but spoke a language unknown to my illiterate grandmother. They probably came from other Italian regions, trying to join the revolutionary groups that were fighting for the unification of the Italian State (then still divided).

My brother and I used to listen with our mouths open and let our fantasies relate all those stories to those we read about in the Italian history books in school; such heroes as Garibaldi and his thousand men, and all the other patriots who fought for the unity of our state. It was amazing!

My grandmother had funny stories about the time she was engaged to be married. There were ways for men to show their love to a lady other than vocal or instrumental serenades, like Romeo and Juliet. My grandmother said that a special lover's whistle woke her up in the middle of the night, and when she looked out the window she saw four or five lighted candles around a funeral-like apparatus. Strange!

In those days, I imagine, the man used unusually special ways to prove his male superiority over the female, and at the same time promised her protection until death, the end. When my grandmother recounted all this, she used to smile, as if she approved of her lover's strange courtship.

Her father was a custodian for the church of San Nicola, located in the "alto la terra" section of town. All daily duties for such a job included cleaning the church in general—including the floor, pews, altar, linens, etc. Also the bells had to be played twice a day, vespers in the afternoon and the Angelus at dawn. Besides all these functions, there was an oil lamp by the altar that had to be kept lit day and night, and for that matter, the oil had to be added continuously and the wick had to be changed very often.

My grandmother, who was about twenty years old then, wore a long gown and an exterior sort of bra sustained by two heavy straps hanging from her shoulders, probably a corset. One summer evening, later than usual, her father told her to go play the Angelus bells and take care of that particular oil lamp.

In the middle of the church there were two uncovered corpses waiting to be buried the next day. The caskets were not used too often yet, and there was an unusual number of dead people due to an epidemic plague mentioned by A. Manzoni in his famous classic book: *I Promessi Sposi*. One of the bodies had half of his face laden with rotten skin.

My grandmother played the bells located in the front of the church. When she came down from the bell tower, it was already dark and she noticed that the lamp, way above the main altar, was very weak and would probably not last through the night and if that happened she would have to face her stepmother's furor.

Reluctantly, she decided to go up to the altar as calmly as she could, without paying much attention to the two caskets not clearly visible because of the darkness. While she added the oil and changed the wick, she heard a rustling-like noise, just like people walking shoeless.

As she started to walk back to the exit, she could see the two corpses and some moving shadows (including her own) on the opposite church wall. Frightened, by accident she tripped on one of the coffins and her hand wound up on that particular body's deformed face. Just before the exit door, one of the straps from the bra latched onto the doorknob. She was now convinced that one of the corpses had grabbed her, so she cried out aloud, "Lasciami! Lasciami! (Let me go! Let me go!)". She broke her strap, and coming out the church she heard, "Baa! Baa!" followed by a bunch of sheep also coming out of the church.

She said that this time she was really scared, but that is questionable because on other occasions she said she dared grown men to resist fear. Along the side of the road to the upper side of town, there was a spot, Fuori Porta, where at night during the summer a group of men sat on a stone wall by the curb, enjoying the breeze of fresh air and at the same time discussing all kinds of things done or to do.

From that side there is a good panoramic view of the main part of the town below, and at night you can see all the lighted lamp posts here and there;. To the left you can also see the complete dark cemetery with tall pine trees and the wall around it. Sometimes small flames like flashlights come and go through the whole area; I imagine it's a chemical reaction from decomposed or cremated bodies—a natural process, but bad enough to cause fear in general.

But not for my grandmother who, for a dime, challenged all those men to go way down there at midnight, and with a lighted candle walk around the whole cemetery. On the scheduled night she did go around the cemetery and all the men saw the candle, but when she was about to walk back she heard a loud man's voice, "Who is there? Who ever you are come forward!" Terrified, she ran back like a thunderbolt. Later she found out about that man—a drunkard by the name of Loreto, who was going home to Poggetello and had missed the main road which is parallel to the one for the cemetery.

During our childhood, we ate solely homemade food. I remember going to the store only to buy salt, sugar, tomato extract and roast coffee. We had our own pasta and bread. Nevertheless, the bread we saw in the local bakery store, to our imagination, was so fascinating that Luigi and I used to ask our grandmother for money to buy that bread. Unreal!

My grandmother, who wore one of those long fan-like gowns, used to insert her right hand into the side of the gown and rummage in a long inner pocket tied to her waist trying to find a nickel. With that, we ran to the bakery in the downtown piazza and not only bought the bread, but also enough lupini (they look like yellow lima beans) for us and our grandmother. My brother and I loved the soup made with minced homemade pasta.

In the winter months, we enjoyed the time the pig was big enough to be killed. Zio Antoniuccio, a friend of our family, did the killing job expertly with the help of strong young men to hold the animal to the ground.

Afterward, they burned the hair with hay and scrubbed the hot skin with rough bricks.

For about a week there was continuous activity in the kitchen where all the body parts of the pig were duly packaged in a special manner: prosciutti, sausages, etc., including the blood. We used to steal little pieces of meat and cook them in the frying pan.

Our grandmother, Nonna, often talked about her favorite son, Francesco, who at the age of about nine was an altar boy in the church of St. Nicola, up the hill from her house. What he liked most was carrying the cross to the cemetery for funerals. After one of those trips, during an awful storm, the boy became very ill. He probably came down with double pneumonia or something. He told his mother he didn't want to die that particular day because he saw too much water in those cemetery graves. He later died in his mother's lap.

A few years later, my grandmother's oldest daughter, Adelaide, mother of three children, also died in her mother's lap. She was about thirty years old. My grandmother always said that she had fourteen children, and the daughter of her first child was the same age as her last daughter, Annina, who was born when my grandmother was fifty years old.

After my grandfather Domenico had died, my grandmother continued all the services as a custodian of

St. Peter's church, such as playing the bells at sundown (the Angelus). Every night she walked down the twelve steps from our kitchen to the street and about one hundred feet to the church across the way, then walked about twenty steps up the bell tower and did the reverse when she finished. For an eighty-old woman, I think that was a lot.

One particular night during the winter, the streets were covered with mixed snow and ice. My grandmother fell. A doctor visited her and said that the hip was damaged and she would not be able to walk for the rest of her life. About a month later, a woman friend of the family, an expert in home made health remedies, visited my grandmother and said that the problem was the knee and if somebody could help her, she could fix it.

That day, my aunt Zia Teresina from Poggetello, a few miles away, came to visit her mother as usual and offered to help in holding my grandmother's leg. At the moment the lady twisted the knee, grandmother got hold of her daughter and shook her so violently as to make her cry like a baby. A few months later, my grandmother got up from bed and was able to walk a few steps at the time with the help of a broom stick.

As I mentioned elsewhere, Zia Teresina, was married to Quirino Di Giampaolo, a bricklayer. They had no children, and that might have been a good reason for them to be very uncomfortable with children's behavior.

Zio Quirino in particular was always in a nervous state of mind and prone to sudden irritability.

I remember very well one day he came over our house when my brother Luigi, who was about six years old, was behaving a little capriciously. My uncle, not being able to make his indisputable speech, took my crying and frightened brother and locked him out onto the bedroom balcony, came back into the kitchen, finished his important dictatorial argument and, about a half hour later, unlocked the balcony door to let my (by then miserable) brother in.

On another occasion, my uncle was putting a new stone floor in the balcony in the front of the house and at one point he needed some kind of tools to move a stone slab from the kitchen next door. My brother Luigi and I were too young to help him. So, he came up with the idea of using the fireplace's blower and my grandmother's broom stick as rollers, so he put them under the slab for transportation. I'll never forget the look on my grandmother's face when she saw her life saving broom stick used for that awful purpose and to top it all off, it broke right in the middle. My brother and I ran away from the house to avoid the macabre scenario between two biggest characters in the family.

The year the Italian people voted for democracy, my grandmother went to the polls and made a beautiful cross on the ballot. She felt so proud to express her own opinion in that very simple manner. However, she was very popular in St. Peter's parish where she volunteered for some activities such as being a godmother to quite a few needy children.

Another little old lady often came over our house. We kids called her Zia Maddalena. She always took the seat by the fireplace, on the opposite side of my grandmother. Most of the time they talked about their dead husbands, while busily knitting. Sometimes I had trouble understanding some of the words they used because they were not compatible to our then-modern education system. They used idioms close to either Latin or French languages as a consequence of the rules imposed by the French Bourbonic King the previous century.

During the 1940-1945 war, World War II, an aerial bombing took place in a wooded area near our home where some German trucks were parked. All the empty shells fell on the roofs of the houses in the whole area. On that particular day, Zia Maddalena took the seat by the little window on the right side of the fireplace, while my grandmother sat by the bigger window on the left side. As soon they heard the noise of the shells, they simultaneously shut both windows closed, as to prevent some kind of danger coming in from the outside.

In the last few years of her life, my grandmother demanded compliments and constant attention that sometimes compromised the position of people who were taking care of her. She played good parts, using simple lies in order to get attention from whom she expected occasional, special treatment.

Here is an example: two of my grandmother's daughters, Luisa and Annina, were living in the United States, and the third one, Teresina, lived in Poggetello. They were in continuous contact with their mother at least by mail or occasional visits; but the person who really took care of my grandmother was my stepmother Concetta, who had enough patience, courage, and plenty of good will worthy of a genuine saint. Especially during last few years when my grandmother lost control of the simplest sanitary functions, I think Zia Concetta must have had an iron stomach.

When my aunts asked their mother how was she doing, my grandmother didn't hesitate to complain about not getting enough attention, especially about food. Zia Teresina, as I said earlier, came to see her mother every Thursday after food shopping (it was the town's market day).

On one of these visits, I remember my grandmother had just finish eating a voluminous bowl of coffee and milk with two big slices of toasted bread. When my aunt was coming up to the kitchen, her mother recognized her steps and called out, "Is that you, Teresina?" "Yes, it's me," said my aunt, coming over by the side of the fireplace. As she put down the shopping bag on the floor, she asked her mother: "How are you today? Did you eat?" My grandmother, right then and there said, "What? Are you kidding? Nobody has given me anything!" All the while keeping an eye on the shopping bag, were my aunt retrieved some fruit.

It was a good thing that I happened to witness everything, and in doing so was able to avert useless gossip and above all, avoid false impressions of Zia Concetta's more than fair reputation.

Luigi and I slept in a bed in the same room as my grandmother's and during the night she complained continuously. I was very busy in school and usually went to bed very late in order to finish all my assignments. My brother Luigi used to put the cushion over his head and somehow was able to sleep while I had a lot of difficulty falling sleep specially during exam time.

I remember getting up in the middle of the night, walking over to my grandmother's bed and asking her, "Nonna! What is the matter?" She said, "Oh, God, help me! I have pains everywhere!" and ran her hand over her thighs and legs. I knew very well that she wanted attention from me, so I just touched her big toe and said, "Is it any better?" She answered, "Oh yes, much better! Thank you! God bless you! Here, I'm saying the rosary for your mother! Ti nostra amen, ti nostra amen, etc." On and on all night long. The big rosary beads passed continuously over the index finger of her right hand, causing a visible cavity just before the nail.

She often said that before marriage she came from the parish of St. Nicola, while her husband lived in a house across from the church of St. Egidio, almost at the top end of town. (The church is now closed because it is not safe.) She also said that her husband's family nickname was "Middio". To this day I am not able to find out more, except that he had two sisters: Angela and Giuseppa.

Emilio and Maria DeSanctis on their Wedding Day

Maria DiGiuseppe DeSanctis

This photograph of my mother was taken in the hospital in Rome.

Innocenzo and Chiara DiGiuseppe with Family Members

This is a photograph of my maternal grandparents with some members of their family. The last girl on the right is my mother. The boy is my Uncle Giuseppe who died while training in the equestrian police.

Domenico and Maria Casale DeSanctis

Luigi and Joe DeSanctis

Don Gaetano Tantalo

(Photo source: Public Domain)

Rose and Joe DeSanctis on their Wedding Day

PART TWO

MY ADOLESCENCE, 1933-1942

CHAPTER SIX

Stories From My Youth

Well! Where was I?

After a brief description of some of the family members who contributed to my character formation during my childhood, I am ready to continue on my fantasy trip through my young age with all the pros and cons involved in it. It might not be a chronological age process but, I am sure it will be a mixture of drama and comic strips.

The first few years after my mother's death, my father was changing considerably. He was losing weight. The enormous amount of work for the only postman in that big town, responsibility for his family, bills to be paid, and the deep grief over the loss of his wife put tremendous pressure on his body and mind that drove him to start to drink. I didn't know what to do to help; I was in a big mess myself.

Fortunately, a holy human being came my way this

time: Don Gaetano Tantalo, a new pastor for our almost deserted church. From the instant we met, he took control of my desperate situation and I sincerely thank God for that. My hope returned, and my Christian faith started to build up stronger and stronger in my heart. I was making progress in school, I handled my friends and relatives in a better manner, and I became more interested in music.

The continuous moral support of Don Gaetano made it possible for me to be better in everything—even in helping my father distribute mail in some areas. I became involved in directing a couple of Schola Cantorum in different parishes. I met more people in similar or worse conditions than mine. Somehow, I did not feel desperate anymore. I felt as though my mother did not really die, but spiritually was with me all the time.

My grandmother, now over eighty-five years old, was cooking for us and occasionally making a few minor mistakes here and there that could create problems for us, like allowing soot from the chimney above the stove to fall into the cooking. Three years had passed since my mother died and I think my father by now was planning remarriage for the benefit of the whole household. The names of two ladies came up, but for some reason at the last minute everything was called off. One of them was probably sick and died a few months later.

About this time, as a church custodian I also served most of the Masses. At one particular Sunday Mass, while I was standing by the altar, Don Gaetano announced the forthcoming marriage of my father to a lady whose name I had never heard. I felt so bad, and I could hardly wait for the Mass to end. I ran to my familiar place in the woods as I wanted to sort things out on my own.

About a month later, a new lady took my mother's place. My ego returned. As a grown-up boy, I felt very rebellious about it. My mother's place was usurped, replaced by a stranger. That day, my miserable meeting with myself in the woods was the longest of all of them, but the last. After about three hours, I had no more tears to dry, so I came home expecting the worse.

This is really the last bad emotion I remember. My stepmother, Concetta Franchi, a complete stranger in the beginning, was another special person God had sent my way. She was a simple and deeply emotional human being who understood my justified hostility and handled my situation with excessive respect. She happened to be one of my mother's friends during her childhood and worked at a hotel out of town for many years.

My faith was now much stronger than my feelings and sufferings, and I became more cooperative and very patient. After all, other people were suffering perhaps more than I. Besides, I wanted to be a good example to my brother Luigi, who demanded a lot of attention, was very disobedient, and often mad at everybody.

For a while I tried to be a mediator between my bossy grandmother who would not give up her position as the head of the household, my brother who found it hard to accept the situation, my father who was very annoyed about everything, and my stepmother who was trying very hard to be accepted in that new family. Zia Concetta and I spent many hours sitting by the fireplace, trying to resolve differences the best we knew how. In other words, I learned very early to cooperate like a grownup.

Again, my confidence and trust for a good cause was a big help for my family, and when my stepsister Maria, and my stepbrother Domenico, came along, I acted like a father to them. My stepmother trusted me in handling her children, much younger than me, physically and morally. I remember one time seeing my sister Maria running around the kitchen, and at the same time hiding her right hand behind her back. At first, I thought she was playing some kind of games, but as soon as I caught her by surprise, to my horror I looked at her thumb; half of it was infected! Immediately, I took her to the hospital where the doctor made a painful cleaning and, thank God, was able to save my sister's finger.

On another occasion, my little brother Domenico complained about pain in his lower abdomen, and the doctor said that it was a mild hernia and that he needed a special belt available only in one pharmacy in Avezzano. There were no trains running at that time because of the war, so we had to wait two or three hours before hitch-hiking—getting on the back of a truck full of sand dust, and covering our eyes for most of the ten or more miles trip to buy and fit my brother with that special belt. My tempered patience paid off. My stepmother never forgot my cooperation and later made her own children look up to me as an example of good behavior.

At the age of about ten, I started to take music lessons from one of the best music teachers I have ever met. His name was Don Eustachio Farina and at that time he was a resident in the Franciscan Convent of Oriente, about two miles away from my home. He had convinced my grandfather Domenico, who used to help in the convent on Sundays, to send his grandson over for music lessons as an exchange for the time my grandfather was spending at the convent.

Father Farina was a short and stocky type of man with a heavy baritone voice. One day, and I think the only day he ever lost his patience, he left for a while. I was crying so hard that some of my tears wet the keyboard. Another friar came in—Don Egidio, my mother's first cousin (I found out that day). He asked what was wrong. I pointed to the music in front of me.

"Oh, that? No problem," he said. He sat next to me and played that particular lesson that was so hard for me, and said, "It is very easy! You see?" I never told him, but my disappointment that day turned out to be purely frustrating. "That's not a good way to encourage a child," I thought. But in a way, that helped me to build up my own ego and improve my willingness to continue no matter what.

On one of those trips to the convent for my lessons my brother Luigi came along, and as soon as we left town, two little dogs followed us. One was black and the other brown. They followed us all the way to the church, at least over two miles, and while I went in for my lesson, my brother remained outside with them. About an hour later, I came out and the two puppies were still there playing with my brother. On our way home, they would not go away from us, so we decided to keep the black one and left the brown one in an open field so his mother could find him. Our grandfather didn't like the idea at first, but we promised we would take a good care of him, so he finally agreed.

A few months went by and we noticed a big change in that puppy's behavior. Very often he would bark for no apparent reasons and acted a little abnormally. We didn't know what to do and spoke to a shepherd we knew who said he would be glad to take him if we wanted to give him up. "I need a good dog for my sheep anyway," he said. But a few months later the shepherd complained about missing sheep, so he gave the dog to a horseman who used him to keep intruders away from his stable located a short distance from his house.

By this time, the dog grew to an unusual size and little by little started to instigate the horses. Besides, all the people who had to get up very early in the morning to catch the train to go to work in Rome were afraid to pass by that stable. Soon, that poor animal had to be put away. The horseman said that the dog most have been a result of a dog-wolf relationship. Too bad.

Practically every day in the summer, we boys were busy in a variety of activities: be it singing or playing. It was also great fun going on different trips. At night, we would sit around the kitchen table in Don Gaetano's parochial house, and either read or listen to different stories, especially about ghosts. During the winter after such discussions, it was a nightmare going home.

We were very young and often tested our own courage. One particular night, we were told that an old lady had died the day before and her body was laid in a casket in the center of St. Peter's church next door. We bet ten cents for anybody who would be able to go to the church, walk past the casket, go up the bell tower, go to the attic above the kitchen ceiling, and drop a small rock on the floor as a sign of the accomplished mission, and then come back. All that with the help of a lighted candle.

Nobody would go, so I took my chance. I remember it was past midnight. I walked through the church with my eyes continually fixed on that coffin, went up the choir and then the attic. My candle went out because of the cold air current the instant I opened the attic door. I got panicky, and although I was shaking terribly, I was able to reach for matches I had in my left pants pocket. After a couple of tries, I finally got it lit again and amazingly saw that nothing had changed around me.

I rested a few seconds and then I reached for the little rock I had put in my right pants pocket, and threw it on the floor in the next room. I was scared doing just that, but my friends, sitting stiff on the chairs in the kitchen below, jumped up like a spring from their seats, at the sound of the rock. So Don Gaetano told me when I ran back at lightning speed!

I was making fast progress with music and I practiced the harmonium (a small organ that operates by pumping the needed air with bellows attached to two pedals). We owned two of them; one was full sized and heavier. It was in one of the churches in our custody, permanently. The other, smaller and more portable, was often in the house but definitely needed two people to move it.

One particular day I wanted to practice so badly, but the small harmonium was in the sacristy of St. Peter's, across street from my house. I looked for help for quite a while. I couldn't find anybody, but as I said, I didn't want to miss my practice. I lifted the instrument to the top of the vestment table in the sacristy, aligned my right shoulder with the border of the pedal opening, and with my left hand I pulled the top of the instrument close to my head. I locked my right hand to the left handle above my head and off I went.

I had already opened the door of the sacristy and that of my house; I walked across the street and up the twelve steps to the kitchen and barely made it to the table. I was exhausted, but I made it. I must have been about fourteen years old. To this day I still can't believe I could have done such a thing. I tried again when I was about twenty-something years old and couldn't do it. Mystery! But there is a well-put saying, "Where there is a will, there is a way." How true!

On many occasions during my lifetime I, like a lot of people, came across hard times, problems big and small, and obstacles of many sorts; but the experiences of my younger years helped me to come out as a winner most of the time.

On one of the walking trips we used to take often, we went to Magliano dei Marsi, maybe five miles away. Don Augusto Orlandi (Don Gaetano's best friend) was the new pastor in the main church in the town. Father Orlandi invited us inside the house where I saw a real piano the first time in my life, like the ones I used to see in different magazines. What a beauty! I remember Don Augusto played a beautiful piece: Rondo alla Turca" by Mozart. Was I impressed!

On our way home, Don Gaetano must have noticed my excited state of mind and asked, "Did you like the piano?" "Oh, I love it!" I said. "What about that music?" he asked. "Perfect!" I answered. Then Don Gaetano asked, "If you had the chance to play a piano, how long will it take for you to play that same piece Don Orlandi played?" "Father," I answered, "No more than two weeks!" I was so sure of my willingness and my ability to make such a statement.

A few months later, Don Gaetano was able to get a piano that he said was for his nephew who was few months old, but really, he bought it to test my promise. He placed that piano on the third floor of a house opposite mine, owned by relatives of Don Gaetano's brother-in-law, Adolfo D'Angelo. I crossed the street and went up to that house's third floor every day for at least three hours at a time. After exactly two weeks we went back to Magliano dei Marsi, where I played the Mozart music for Father Orlandi who was extremely surprised.

Another instrument that attracted my attention more or less around this time was the piano accordion, called that because it has a keyboard like a piano for the right hand. I had seen small such instruments with limited numbers of keys and bass notes, used for small rustic dances—polkas and waltzes. Most of the time the same tunes were played over and over. I had never seen a full-size accordion with the standard number of keys for the right hand and enough bass notes for the left hand.

I heard that two brothers, professional accordionists, were residents of Tagliacozzo most of the time: Vezio and Achille Bucci. Some of my friends told me that the two musicians were terrific and promised to find out where we could go to listen to either one of them.

Naturally, Don Gaetano found out, and to my amusement he arranged a friendly meeting with one of the brothers at his brother-in-law's house, a couple of houses up the street from mine. What I saw that night was the most beautiful thing I could ever imagine. I remember Achille played a march, *Sharpshooter*, with real magnificence—and what can I say about all the passages with his left hand over all those buttons? Unbelievable reality!

After he finished, Mrs. D'Angelo invited him and the rest of us for coffee in the adjoining kitchen. While they were talking, I asked permission to go to the other room and look at the instrument. It didn't take long for me to figure out the bass system of the instrument (thanks to the harmony theory I learned from Father Farina). After few minutes, I was able to play a couple of simple songs, although I had a little problem with moving the bellows smoothly with the keyboard positioned vertically. I fell in love with the accordion instantly.

I was told that a fellow friend, Franco Pappalardo, had bought an accordion recently; he worked in Rome and came home on weekends. So every Saturday night I waited patiently for him at the railroad station. I knew that he would invite me over to his house and while he was eating his supper, I would practice the accordion. It worked out beautifully for a while.

Later I was able to get a medium-size instrument (eighty bass) in more or less fair condition. I told my friend Toto Cervellieri, the photographer, "Someday I will be able to buy a nice-looking accordion just like the one the Bucci brothers play!" He said, "As soon as the war ends we both will go to Rome and shop around." About a year later he called me and said that he had to go to Rome for his own business, and while there he visited one music store and saw a beautiful accordion for fifteen thousand lire.

The week after, we both went to Rome and I took with me nineteen thousand lire to make sure I had enough money to buy the instrument Toto had seen. But the price changed to twenty-one thousand lire in less than a week. "I'm coming back next week," I told the owner.

We went back with twenty-five thousand lire and again the price was jacked up to thirty thousand lire. "This can't be!" I thought. We went back in two weeks for the last time with thirty-five thousand lire. No way! The price was already thirty-nine thousand lire. So, we both gave up. The war had just ended and quite a few items were being exported at much better prices than we could afford in Italy. My father felt badly about it and a few years later he traveled to north Italy to buy a beautiful instrument with my name engraved on it, and shipped it to me in New York.

The accordion opened for me a busy schedule of activities and opportunities to meet a lot of people. As a portable instrument, it is possible to accompany groups of people or choirs not necessarily in church, church halls, or other places equipped with an organ or piano. Most importantly, it retains the standard tone compatible with other wind instruments, because the piano usually goes out of tone quite often.

We often went on pilgrimages to places like the Holy Trinity Sanctuary, four hours away on foot. I carried the accordion strapped to my shoulders: a practical organ replacement. I also started to play it for dances called Veglioni, with three, four, or sometimes five musicians.

One particular rainy day in March, we were engaged to play out of town in the town of Petrella Liri (about a two-hour walking trip). I covered my accordion with a rain coat and started to walk around one o'clock in the afternoon. We arrived at our destination after three, all soaking wet.

We started to play right then and there, and about an hour later we were offered a big glass of wine to drink on an empty stomach. Not a very nice treat, but it helped to warm our bodies. Stiff from the cold rain, at about one a.m. we finished our job, and the dance committee assigned each one of us musicians to different houses for supper and a bed for the night.

I wound up in a house that had the first floor used as a bar or cantina, where a lot of men were drinking and playing cards around a long table. I remember it was Friday, and the host put a dish of tuna fish in the middle of that table and motioned to me to start to eat. "I'm not hungry," I said, and he showed me the way upstairs to the bedroom. His wife must have noticed my embarrassment of not wanting to eat in front of everyone, and brought that dish up to my bedroom later.

Most of the time we played for our own sports center, Casa Balilla, in downtown Tagliacozzo with Mario Romano on the trombone, Nestore Gentile on the trumpet, Pietro Trovato on the saxophone, Vinicio Morgante on the guitar, Guido Maiolini on another saxophone, and Toto Cervellieri on the violin.

Those Veglioni sometimes lasted eight hours, and I was the only one who lived in the upper part of the town (Sulla Terra). My friends often offered to accompany me home. I refused all the time, but I was scared thinking about passing in front of a particular house where, according to what people said, a man changed into a wolf during the night and attacked people. Though I never saw anything, I did hear noises —stone pieces running through the street and a lot of cries from cats—and that was enough to be scared of anyway!

We also played in Scurcola Marsicana, at the Count Veduli's mansion. Beautiful place! On many occasions, the Count himself came dressed up in what I could call a royal uniform. We became very popular and made headlines in the local newspapers.

We played for fancy weddings and for the rich farmers of Fucino in Avezzano. In addition to a small fee, we were able to take home good food not yet available to the public in general because of the war. I remember a good violin player, Prof. De Giorgi, showing up for the job with the violin wrapped up in a medium-size sack, because the wood case was broken, he said. By the end of the night he came home with the sack full of food on his shoulder and the violin under his arm. The poor man had seven kids to feed!

With the exception of the few music lessons I received from Father Farina, I kept going on my own, and I got a big help from Don Gaetano. He didn't play the keyboard because of an accident on his arms during his college years, but he had a powerful musical knowledge —from Gregorian chant and complicated solfeggio passages to harmony expressions of great masters like Mozart, Chopin and Beethoven.

Every time he listened to classical music, he described his feelings just like a magic brush in the hands of great artists like Michelangelo. His inspiration helped me to go in the right direction. One day I surprised him by playing his favorite Mozart Sonata in C, without the sheet music. Not long after, he arranged a meeting with a local veterinarian and violin player who invited over to his house a famous pianist, Prof. Giorgi, retired from a busy career as a pianist for the royal family in Australia, now living in the neighboring town of Scurcola Marsicana.

After a friendly introduction, Don Gaetano asked Prof. Giorgi if he could kindly listen to my playing. "By all means," said Giorgi. So, I played that Mozart Sonata, all ten pages, from memory. I was very timid, but very proud to have finished without mistakes of any sort. When I turned around, expecting at least a good sign of approval, to my disbelief, I saw the professor shaking his head like a discontented person would do.

My imagination collapsed like the Trojan horse; I didn't know what to say. Don Gaetano noticed my embarrassment and anxiously waited for an explanation. "Not one note is missing, but the phrasing is very poor. It is like reading a beautiful long letter without breathing, and all your fast runs are not uniform," he said. "What would you suggest to correct all these bad habits?" asked Don.

The Professor got up, walked over the piano,

positioned his right thumb on the C key and said, "This!" He played the five keys: C-D-E-F-G, one at the time, very slowly and heavily. He raised each finger to the same height and applied the same amount of pressure on each key. "And everything you play from now on, you will practice this way first!" he continued.

That was another one of the best music lessons I ever had.

As human beings, we are not perfect and neither are our hands and fingers. If we put our hands on the table not too flat, and we try to raise each finger as high as we can while keeping pressure on the other four, we notice that the thumb, the index finger, the middle finger and the pinkie will go very high, while the ring finger will barely go one inch high. That explains the uneven touch of the keys. By doing the exercises the professor suggested, I was able not only to control the same amount of pressure on each key, but reinforce the ring finger as well.

They say that Chopin was obsessed about the weakness of his ring fingers and was convinced that the two fingers were tied to the pinkies, because if we try to raise the pinkie at the same time as the ring finger in the example I mentioned above, both fingers will rise with no problem. One day Chopin tried to cut the nerves between the two fingers with a razor blade. He was rushed to the hospital just in time. (Editor's note: This story may actually be about Robert Schumann and not

Frederic Chopin.)

I spent my pre-teenage years mostly involved in music related circumstances either in Schola Cantorum rehearsals and performances or private and public dances, mostly within my birth town, Tagliacozzo. I remember giving a recital on the piano in the local Talia theater, but I don't recall the piece I played. It was enough fun to smooth out the bitter memory of my mother.

Besides the physical education program after school, our city also had other free programs for young people and one of them was a night music course for marching band training. I joined, and after about six months of solfeggio only, the band leader, Rubeo, gave us the choice of instruments we wanted to play. I choose the clarinet in Eb, which is half the size of a standard Bb clarinet. It was a lot of fun!

Our first appearance took place about a year later on New Year's Day, in the public stand of the city square. I remember playing a short clarinet solo part in Verdi's first opera, *Oberto, Conte di San Bonifacio*. I did very well!

The night before, we wanted to surprise some rich families that contributed to the band's fund with our well rehearsed serenade. It was a very cold night, and we rehearsed one more time before going out. By the time we were supposed to play, our own saliva froze in the mouthpiece. All the squeaky sounds were really ridiculous. It was a complete flop! But we had a lot of fun.

We learned three complete marches by heart, and by the summer we were hired to play for a religious feast in Celano dei Marsi, a city not too far from us. We started to go around town to play those three marches on different streets. The band leader would show with his fingers which march we had to play, numbers one, two or three, and the people admired our repertoire. We were really making a good impression, so we played more marches, numbers four, five and six, which meant numbers one, two and three again. By the time the day was over, they noticed our tricks and we had to leave town fast.

I continued my music activities with the accordion by serenading people or playing for small house parties. All my teenage friends liked the happy feelings I was generating with that magic instrument, and soon they started to organize various escapades. On one occasion, they prepared a well-done meal of a roast and potatoes that I really enjoyed. Right after we finished, in unison they chanted, "Mew! Mew! Mew!" So, the roast was a cat.

On another occasion, they gave me an extra dose of wine and made me go through the whole town, playing and singing. We wound up in a hotel's dining room and ate donkey meat. I remember it was Saturday because the next day, Sunday, I played Masses in three different churches and the people complimented me on my amazing performance of the previous night in different town locations. All I remember was what they had given me at the beginning of the night.

With my friends Vinicio on the guitar, and Toto on the violin, we serenaded people on their name day. On one occasion, we were still out after curfew time. About two o' clock in the morning, we finished playing our last song and decided to go home. We heard heavy steps approaching our way and we knew they were German soldiers by the sound of their wooden shoes.

We ran as quietly as we could and hid behind a huge pile of wooden logs. Holding our breath, we heard them getting closer and closer and all of sudden they stopped. They found our hiding place very easily because Vinicio's guitar was sticking out and shining from the lamp post across away. At first the two soldiers aimed their machine guns at us, but when they saw the instruments they changed their attitudes and made us play more songs for their own pleasure.

Our best night for serenading was in the month of January, exactly on the seventeenth, feast of St. Anthony the Abbott. Our list of people by the name of Anthony was quite long, and that made us very busy all night long. We received lot of gifts based mostly on different kinds of pastries. Most of the time we had no place to put them, so we used the instruments cases. Vinicio put his share inside the guitar box, making the instrument almost inaudible. We had a ball!

During the war, and at exactly the same time Monte Cassino in south Italy collapsed, a lot of German soldiers retreated to the north in a hurry, and some of them passed my town on their way to Rome and the vicinity.

One particular day, I had gone to our small vineyard for a little clean up job and on my way home I passed in front of Toni Barbante's house. From the street, I could hear loud male voices and I knew that only Toni's wife and their two daughters should have been in there. Toni saw me from the kitchen window and called me over. I walked in and saw two German soldiers in the familiar S.S. uniform. "Please keep me company," Toni said. "These two soldiers came in and I realized they are tired and drunk at the same time. I am a little worried about the women!"

Fortunately, they had an accordion and I asked them if I could play it. They agreed. I played a few Straus waltzes. They liked them so much, they continued their drinking and left the house in a very happy mood, just before dark. I don't think I did a superb job, but Toni never forgot the blessing of my musical help in that particular day.

During my school years at the Magistral Institute in Avezzano, sometimes we had to wait two hours before boarding the train for the trip back home from school. I was lucky to meet an elderly couple who lived near the school on Via 20 Settembre; and they had a beautiful accordion that they didn't know how to play. I played it instead for their entertainment and my own practice as well, a few hours every week.

In 1943, right after the school closed, Avezzano was hit by a powerful air strike and for quite a while was isolated and cut off completely from any form of school activities. Only a couple of years later was I able to take a trip and see the damage. To my horror I saw no house standing on the block where that elderly couple lived. To this day I don't know if they were able to escape that catastrophe. There was no sign of my school building either.

Just before that bombing, one morning my classmates and other school friends waited for me at the railroad station with an accordion, and made me go around Avezzano playing and accompanying their singing spree. I don't think that was an appropriate time to do such a thing, but, as I said before, we were young and immature.

The principal of the liceo, or school, Mr. Nardelli went around all the classes of the day asking for information about "that reckless individual that went around the city playing the accordion." All my friends kept quiet because they were part of that miserable improvised troupe. We got away with it!

* * *

In the spring of 1942, I finished the first year of Superior Magistral School's three-year course and because of the war, my class of 1923 was scheduled for military duties. At the beginning of the summer, the government called all the young men born in the first six months of 1923, and planned on calling the rest of the boys in the fall. At the same time, a ministerial decree came out, allowing all the students in the last year of school to finish the course and graduate; they would be called for military duties the following year.

I was born in December, the second part of the year. Naturally I thought of trying to skip a year by studying really hard during the summer and then take the admission examinations in the fall, before my military call. I did the best I could with the help from Don Gaetano and in September I took the test which lasted one full week.

For one particular oral session, I had Professor Nardelli (the one who was looking for the reckless musician awhile back), and a woman, a professor of philosophy. I had a textbook with me just in case! They asked me some history questions and at the same time information on my background. I happened to mention music and that opened a magical door for them, but mostly for me.

The bells of the nearby cathedral started to play, bringing back good memories of their younger age full of unforgettable songs, their wedding memoirs, etc.

Naturally, to my own amusement, I had plenty of time to take furtive looks at my book for the right answers. They did ask for them later, and after I finished they approved of what I said with a sly smile.

I was promoted to the third year and when my call came I was granted the permission to finish my school year. The very first day of school in October, I met Professor Nardelli on the steps to the second-floor classes. "Your name please?" he asked. "DeSanctis," I answered. "Oh! You are the one who skipped a year! I remember now!" So he did, and for the whole year we had Latin and Italian literature with him, and he picked on me practically every week.

One particular day, I didn't have time to go over a history topic and on the train, I asked my friend and classmate Duilio Marini about it, and he told me all he had read in his pocket-size book written by an author named Foffano. As soon as we took our seats at our desks, the professor called my name. "Tell the class about Giambattista Vico and his work!" he said. I told all I knew from my friend Marini, and that was not enough for him.

"What book did you use?" he demanded. "A book by Mr. Foffano!" I answered. "Oh!" he said. "That's just wonderful, Mr. Foffano! I'll call you that name from now on!" So, he did—the whole year. In every class I had with him, I felt terror and madness at the same time. My desk mate, Pietro Di Rocco, to this day tells me he remembers seeing my face turn very pale every time Nardelli entered our class.

In the month of May, an order came from the state department to close the school early because of the war, and all the teachers were disappointed, especially Mr. Nardelli who had been so busy ridiculing my Foffano personality for so long, and didn't have enough material to scrutinize each student individually; so he had to do a mass interrogation on all his subjects.

I'll never forget one particular Monday at the end of May, we had a Latin syntax mass examination first thing in the morning. Mr. Nardelli started to call students in alphabetical order to the blackboard where he had written a difficult Latin syntax phrase to be translated, and nobody seemed to know the answer. It was a tricky surprise for the whole class and as the students with A, B and C initial names piled up in front of the board, I took a fast look at the text book we had and to my unbelievable surprise, that phrase was in it, translation and all.

"Oh! Now!" he sang, "Let's hear from Mr. Foffano!" For the first time in months I felt exuberant, I felt real revenge. I ran to the board and wrote the translation like a rescue hero. "Oh God! This is a miracle! All this time I never knew that DeSanctis was the best of this class!" he stated. At once I became an idol and from that moment on, even if I said baloney it was great for him. At last I was glad to be in that class that only lasted another week.

In Avezzano I met a very good trumpet player, Nestore Gentile, and we became very close friends. We played together for ballroom dances in the main cinema building in town. We played mostly all the American tunes of the 1940's we heard from the radio. It was a brilliant experience.

After the American landing at Anzio, I decided to find out my possibilities of admission to Rome's St. Cecilia Conservatory of Music. One day I went to the admissions office and asked for an application. A lady offered to help, and after I gave her my name and address, she asked what was my voice range, "Tenor, baritone, or what?"

"But I'm applying for composition," I said. "Well, you gave me the impression of being an aspiring singer!" she said. After I signed that paper and paid the appropriate fee, she gave me the date of my audition required for admission, which was set for the following week.

On the day of that audition, I left Tagliacozzo by train at four a.m. in order to be at the conservatory building at eight a.m. sharp. At about 8:30 I was taken into a big hall with huge antique wood arm chairs lined up against the walls and filled with distinguished imposing gentlemen with long beards who reminded me of Verdi, Garibaldi, and other bearded personalities of the eighteenth century.

A little frightened, I took a seat at the only desk in the center of the room. One of the gentlemen told me that my audition consisted of reading aloud in the solfeggio manner, using my hand for the appropriate beat, the paper in front of me at the desk; and I was given a half an hour's time to look at it first.

That piece of music was thirty-two bars long, made up with all types of notes and rests, in five or six different keys and each bar with different time signature. I started to read it and I went past the half page when I came across a three eight measure filled with four eight notes. "This is impossible!" I said to myself. "How on earth could I beat my hand three times and count four notes within?" I asked! All my dreams collapsed at that very moment. I got up and walked right out the exit door.

I heard some of those men calling me back but I had made up my mind. There was nothing I could do about what I had seen. I took the train back home very upset and just before I reached town all of sudden it hit me. It was the easiest part of the whole exam. The three eight beat is faster than regular three fourths, for that reason I didn't have to beat my hand three times but only once and name all four notes evenly just like a triplet. I should have called it a quadruplet. A very simple task that could only happen to self-taught people. Anyway, the damage was already done and I felt miserable about it for awhile and let everything become a memory.

One of my friends from school, an expert in Italian Literature, told me one day that he was trying to write a drama based on patriotic actions which took place in Italy about the year 1850. He asked me if I was willing to write the music for it. I said, "I'm new in the field." "So am I," he said. "We both will try!" "In that case let's try," I concluded. He gave me an idea of the play and every couple of weeks he gave me some lyrics.

As I finished each melody, he would borrow the music for a day or two but didn't tell me why. Finally, he gave me the ending chorus to compose. I did and the same thing happened. He borrowed it and gave it back to me a week later. This time I asked him what had he done with my music. He said: "I hope you don't mind if I tell you now that I showed your music to Mr. Vincenzo Bellezza, one of the best orchestra conductors in Rome, and he liked it. He said that the chorus has somewhat of religious feelings in it!" "Wonderful!" I said. "What is patriotic for me is also religious. And I think I am right on that!" I guessed he didn't like that so he commissioned another musician for the chorus.

That melodrama was presented in our local Talia Theater, bearing one name for the words and two for the music. Even though the play went fairly well, I lost interest in it and as soon as everything was over I took my music back and let all that also become a memory. I confess that I was a little upset about it for the simple reason that he didn't stick to his initial pact. All of sudden he thought that his work was a masterpiece while mine was being criticized behind my back.

After my mother died, my friends filled up the emotional vacuum I felt, maybe because some of them were in the same situation I was. My friend Elio Giovagnorio had recently lost his father in the United States, and was the only child now living with his mother. Another friend, Antonio Verna, had lost his father a week after he was born, in a strange incident.

According to an old local tradition, January 17th, feast of St. Anthony the Abbot, all the men by that name received a special treat, be it a serenade or improvised party, in which everybody also participates and get what they called "la pagnottella", sort of a Halloween's trick or treat. My friend, Antonio (Toni) Verna's father's name was also Antonio, and he worked for the railroad. On January 17, 1923, he and three co-workers by the name of Anthony also, went to Poggetello, using a small railroad cart.

They visited some friends for the happy occasion, and on their way back, a little drunk and naturally not aware of railroad activities, their cart collided with an oncoming train and all of them died instantly. My friend, born the week before, was given the name of Vincent. His mother, right after the accident, changed his name to Anthony like his father.

We felt like we were sharing the same fate that created a bond of solid friendship way back to our elementary school years. We shared our dreams of growing up to be either actors, pilots or travelers to fantastic places like South America or Australia. But most of the time we spent looking at the sun that never seemed to go down. We were in a hurry to grow up fast.

We used to go down to the railroad station and watch trains full of young boys heading for the army headquarters and we wondered, "When are we going to be like them?" During the summer, we were supposed to go into the woods nearby and pick up as many dried pine cones as we could so that our parents could use to start up either the fireplace or the brick oven in the winter. Instead we took with us any length of old rope we could find and tied it between two tree trunks for an improvised swing over a very deep, steep terrain.

When the swing came backward, the rope touched the ground, while forward the rope was as high as 15 feet. One day, Toni tried it first and did fine, but when my turn came, I secured my right foot in the rope from behind while my left foot slid, leaving me suspended in the air with my right foot caught in the rope, swinging at the same time and dragging my head along the incline. Fortunately, I didn't get hurt because that spot had high grass.

After a good laugh, my friend got on the swing again

and had a grand time. When my second turn came, I got on very carefully and started to enjoy it very much. All of sudden, the old patched up rope snapped on the left side of me, sending my body sliding violently into the tree. Somehow, I held my left knee with my left hand before falling. This time we didn't laugh. Toni felt very bad and I escaped with a few scratches on my right arm and both legs.

Although we didn't practice any sport in particular, we liked soccer, and on Sunday afternoons we went to the soccer field near the railroad and stood on the left side of the field to watch our friend Enniuccio play the left wing on our town team. We knew he was the best player, but he had a little problem with his father who disliked the game so much that on some occasions he hid his son's shoes. But one day one of the father's friends dragged him to the field just in time for him to see his son scoring a goal.

From that day on he went to every single game his son played, he would stand on the left side of the field where his son was and encouraged him in a peculiar way! He yelled to his son, "If you don't win, you better not come home tonight!" Very funny!

One day, my grandfather told me that I talked in my sleep and he could not make out what I was saying. He also told me that he saw me getting up from bed, walking around the room and then going back to bed, always with my eyes closed. I thought that had to do with the excitement of the multiple activities of the day, especially during the summer vacation from school.

The first time I took part in a pilgrimage to the Holy Trinity chapel (a good four-hour trip on foot, up in the mountains) even though I rode my uncle's donkey for a while, when I came home I slept for good forty-eight hours. During that long sleep, I dreamed of going back on the same trip, the same way. But here is what I really did: I got up from bed as I was getting off the donkey and walked the length of our bedroom that we shared with our grandparents, my father's bedroom and the kitchen and back to bed when my uncle helped me back on the donkey again.

Another time I dreamed that my friend Toni Verna and I were sitting on the steps of my house's front door, talking more or less about our plans for the upcoming summer. A street vendor, selling clothing material rolled up on his shoulders, for advertisement purpose, screamed, "Bella tela musolina!" (This means "beautiful muslin cloth".) Right then and there we decided to follow him, because it seemed a promising trade.

Here is what I really did: I took the sheet and blanket from our bed, rolled up, walked to my grandparents' bed and yelled, "Bella tela musolina!" once, and deposited the whole roll on their bed. It was the month of June, not too warm specially at night. About two in the morning, my brother Louis was looking for the blanket in both sides of our bed, while my grandparents were complaining about being too hot.

A few years later, I joined my friends Arnaldo and Elio and left town to go to work for a construction company that was building a dam, over the Velino river, to generate electricity for Terni's central power. We boarded a big farm house in Casette, near Rieti and close to our place of work. We slept in the big room upstairs that had six beds: three for us, one for Arnaldo's father, and the other two for the work leader Romeo and his son.

My first job was operating a machine that turned big soft rocks into a sort of gravel to be used for concrete mix. It was my new experience in that type of work and I liked it. After a few weeks, my friends started to tease me about my talking in the sleep and that made me a little uncomfortable. I told my superior about and he gave me another job at night, operating a water pump that cleared the river bed of any amount of water which accumulated during the night, so it would be possible for the morning crew to work in it.

The pump was not too far from the farm house. I could come back every few hours when the amount of water accumulated was minimal and I could stop the pump for a while, and then restart it as soon as more water went in. There were no lights anywhere in sight and I had a gas lamp with me lighted all the time. The first few nights weren't too bad, maybe because I came across a book, *Crime and Punishment* by Tolstoy. It was very interesting and I felt less solitude while the other five men slept peacefully.

One particular night I read the episode of the student murdering those two ladies, and the description was so real and impressive that it frightened me to the point of not willing to venture out. After calming down a little, I decided reluctantly to go out and start the pump. I sat on a rock while the pump was running. Looking at the amount of water accumulated in the river bed I planned on staying out there for maybe ten more minutes. It was now half past one in the morning and all of sudden the lamp ran out of gas. "This can't be!" I said to myself, and left the pump running. I ran inside the house, up to the second floor, filled the lamp with gas and lighted it.

Instantly I heard, "Stop that pump! Boy!" I turned around in a flash and saw Antonio, sitting in bed with his right-hand index finger pointed at me yelling again: "You! You! Stop that pump!" As I had turned, the lamp's hook caught the sleeve of my shirt and fell on the floor and started to burn my pants. "Oh God!" I thought that was the end of me. "This is too much!" I concluded, and after putting the flame out, went to bed.

The pump ran on empty part of the night and of course, burned down. The next day I was called into the manager's office for the expected lecture, but I was satisfied to prove that after all I wasn't the only one who talked in his sleep.

In order for us to go in town for shopping or the like, we had to cross the Velino river by a small boat tied to a wheel that ran on a steel rope secured on both sides of the river. Parallel to that rope, there was another steel rope which we pulled to get the boat across either way. The private property on both sides of the river had beautiful inviting ripe white grapes and big black figs, but it was continually guarded by the owners armed with rifles. My friend Arnaldo suggested we could try to get some of those beautiful fruits at night. Less conspicuous.

We did try that, a couple of days after, on a very clear autumn night. We did get some, but we got caught, mainly because Arnaldo used a flashlight to pick the best. We heard a gunshot and ran as fast as we could to the boat and stayed put in the middle of the river because the owner on the other side's property was also yelling. That boat was very useful but could also be a nightmare if you needed it in a hurry and happened to be on the other side. One night, my friend Elio was all by himself and after waiting more than an hour for somebody to bring the boat over, decided to cross the river via the suspended rope with both hands and legs. He did but lost his wallet with all his money and identification papers.

In the few months we spent on that job, we made some local friends and sometimes they invited us to their homes. One Sunday afternoon, we were invited for a house party in nearby town of Casette. It was a beautiful isolated house with plenty of property around it. We walked in and didn't see any food in the kitchen or in the dining and living rooms. After we took a seat, the host excused himself and left the house for few minutes. When he came back, he had two big round watermelons, one in each arm.

He cut the two watermelons in half and with a special carving knife. He cut around the inside skin, then cut the whole inside in small pieces. Next, he went down the basement, and came back with two bottle of sweet muscatel wine and emptied them on all the four halves, gave us a fork, and said, "Please, help yourselves!" It was delicious! We had never tasted anything like it in our lives, mainly because our climate in Abruzzo is colder then Rieti and unable to produce such a beauty and yet only a few miles away.

My work leader, Romeo, could not read or write very well, but had a perfect memory about keeping the exact time each man spent on the job. He trusted me to the point of helping him call out the name of each man and write down the amount of work time for each and every night. He remembered all the details and nobody ever complained.

I spent my secondary school years in the Avviamento Professionale School near the soccer field in my home town, Tagliacozzo. My best friend and classmate in those years was Guido Ciamei. We got along fine and as a matter of fact, at least according to our French teacher Bonaventura Pellacchy, we looked alike. In the three years we spent there, sitting on the same double desk, we were the object of confusion for the teachers and laughter for the classroom. Mr. Pellacchy very often called my name but meant my friend Ciamei or vice versa. The same thing happened with our music teacher, Mr. Liberati.

The entrance door to the house where Ciamei lived with his mother Josephine and his sister Giovanna, was on the street level, leading to the two bedrooms, while the kitchen was down one flight of stairs—an unusual set up! As a routine, every morning I passed on my way to school and knocked at that door and that of my other two friends down the hill: Amore Ornello and Angelo Amicucci. All four of us continued on walking to school, usually talking about what was going on in the war with Abissinia.

If we knew from the radio that the Italian soldiers in Africa occupied any of the towns or villages, that alone could have been a sure excuse for demanding a day off. We would gather as a very conspicuous group and march around town following one student with the flag. A peculiar celebration that sometime took place twice a month.

During one winter, Guido got sick and had to stay home few days. His mother was worried stiff when one day, while she was busy downstairs doing some cooking, her son with a very high fever, got up from the bed and went outside in the street under a heavy rain. We all feared for the worse, but, thank God, he got better in no time at all. Unfortunately, years later he volunteered in the Italian Air Force as a radio-telegraph operator and his plane collided with the tower of Pisa on a training mission. Everybody on board died instantly. A very ironic destiny!

The first year in that secondary school, I failed a course on basic machine shop and my father arranged for me to spend the whole summer in one of his friend's garage: Enea Liberati. I learned to repair flat tires for some of the few cars around the whole zone. On Thursdays, a few people came from nearby villages by bicycle which they deposited in that garage while going to shop. I didn't know anything about riding a bicycle then, but I planned on borrowing one of them in the evening, just before they were picked up.

I remember it was in the month of September, about six p.m. I tried to ride a medium-sized bike and, with the exception of few cases of unsteadiness, I was able to maintain my balance fairly well. After about a mile or so, I decided to turn back by making a U turn without putting my foot down. Unfortunately I didn't make it and I fell, bike and all, in a ditch alongside the highway. Except for few scratches here and there I didn't get hurt seriously, but I noticed painful white bubbles on both my arms and legs and felt the same burning sensation on my face.

Evidently, I wound up in a dense accumulation of poison ivy and naturally got the best reward for my excitement about learning to ride the blessed bicycle. I didn't want people to see me in that miserable condition, so I waited more than an hour before going back to the garage.

The year after, I didn't do too well in the course of basic wood working and again my father talked to one of the carpenters who owned a small shop in town near the railroad station. He specialized in house furniture in general, but sometimes he made expensive coffins. At the end of that summer and about a week before my exams, a young boy about two years old died, and my boss was commissioned to make the appropriate coffin which he shipped to the house as soon as it was ready.

At closing time, he called me over and said that all the other men were very busy finishing an important job, and ordered me to pass by that boy's house on my way home and seal the cover of the coffin as soon as the priest finished the prayers. He handed me six screws and a screwdriver and said, "Here is all you need!" I headed to the house, up the hill about five hundred feet before my house. "Why me?" I said aloud. "This is not the kind of work I am planning on doing in my lifetime!"

I wasn't too worried about doing the work as much as

feeling the pain of the young parents watching me as some kind of evil snatcher. I did it! But I'll never forget the sight of all those people's eyes looking at me, like some kind of thief. I found real pleasure in going back to school and from that point on I became more determined on following a good lead to my future.

Spending my early years with my brother Luigi was an experience of mixed feelings. At that time, he was my only brother and I loved him very much, even though he differed slightly from me in character. He was a little restless. When he was about three years old still wearing a baby outfit, on one Sunday morning during a high mass in our church in St. Peter, he was running around the altar while I was serving the Mass, taking care of a lighted incense holder, and keeping an eye on Luigi all at the same time.

I left the holder on the floor for a few minutes, to serve wine and water to the priest. All of sudden I saw my brother running backwards in the direction of the hot incense holder, and then he sat on it. My warning plea was nothing compared with his screams from pain. He suffered severe burns on his rear end and cried constantly for the whole week.

During cold winter nights, we used a copper container device filled with red hot charcoal to warm up the bed before going to sleep. One night, my brother Luigi didn't come to bed at the same time I did.

Naturally, when he did his side was cold. He was upset and went back to the fireplace and burned more wood and later filled up that heating device and nervously moved it around his side of bed. I was in a pleasantly sound sleep when I felt a sharp pain on my right leg, and that sent me running through the whole house, crying like a baby. Luigi had pushed that instrument directly into my leg. I saw stars alright and thanks to my grandmother's friend Assunta, who applied a sort of ointment on my leg, I was able to go back to school in a week.

About this time, I got very sick and had to stay in bed for few days with a fever. One evening, my mother and my grandmother went to church after putting some potatoes to roast in the fireplace. Nobody was home for about an hour or so. I ran a very high fever that unconsciously made me get up from bed, walk into the kitchen two rooms away, and uncover the tin pan in the fireplace. They panicked over what I had done and for sure they thought my end was imminent. But to everybody's unexpected surprise, when the doctor came the next morning, my fever was gone.

My grandfather, often took me to visit our small vineyard, (about a mile away from our home) and the old farm house next to it. On the ground floor, there were three large basins, each connected to individual wells which were used to process the grapes to make wine during harvest time, usually in the fall. As many as three families could use those basins at the same time, and while handymen carried the grapes from the field, each family had somebody to keep an eye on the pile of grapes for fear of mutual stealing.

One year, my grandfather put me in charge of our grape pile, while another family had a very old man watching theirs. I remember having a lot of fun going in and out the building and teasing that poor man who was wearing an earring on his left ear and could hardly walk with the help of a cane, trying to catch up with my hide-and-seek game. What a miserable way to have fun! When that old man died, my friend Toni and I went to visit him. His face was covered with a white sheet, and we knelt down by the left side of his bed and joined the rest of the people saying the rosary. A woman came in after we did, walked over to the dead man and uncovered his face. Toni and I looked at the earring and started to laugh so loudly that we had to leave the place quickly enough to avoid any beating from any of those people.

During the 30's, Zio Pietro, my father's only brother who crossed the Atlantic seven times to go to work in the United States, decided to retire and finally returned to Italy for good. I remember admiring his thick mustache and his sharp brown suit with a pocket watch connected to the front of his vest. His retirement didn't last too long and after about a month or so he went to one of the fairs and bought himself a very wild donkey and started farming again just like the old times.

His two boys were in college at that time and sometimes he asked me to help him make a few trips to his farm and back to the house with that donkey, but warned me not to get behind it at any time. Not long before, we had a little female donkey in my family and it was so calm, my brother and I played with it like a toy. Nothing like the one my uncle bought—it looked too wild to me, and too smart for a donkey. Its ears were always straight up like a rabbit and would come down only at the sound of my uncle's voice. It was amazing for me to witness that! I did make a few trips without incidents of any sort. I took my uncle's advice seriously and pulled the animal's halter and kept my distance most of the time.

In our farmhouse, we had two big bundles of dried grape branches which we could use to start up the fireplace or the oven to bake bread. My father asked my uncle if we could borrow the donkey just for one trip to pick up those branches and my uncle told my father to send me over to the stable the next day to get the donkey. Early the next morning I went to my uncle who told me to ride the donkey, because the trip was a little too long for me and by now the animal knew me well. He said, "Just in case it would show a little hostility, don't be afraid to scold it and if necessary use a stick!"

I took his advice and rode the donkey right from the start. Everything was going well as far as going down the hill, then some level ground and up part of another hill. We came across a short flat spot and the donkey stopped intentionally. I used the stick and scolded it a couple of times with no results whatsoever. Its ears remained rigid and its head straight up. There was no use; he knew that my uncle wasn't the one riding it.

I didn't realize what could happen and just touched the donkey one more time with the stick. Before I knew it, I found myself face down on a bush fence with all kinds of scratches on my face and both of my arms. Thank God, nothing very serious. Mad and furious as I could be, I got hold of the halter, continued the rest of the trip by keeping a good distance to avoid the worst, I reached the farmhouse and was able to tie the halter to the farmhouse's door handle.

Inside the house I found a very long pole that was used to get the chestnuts from out of the reach tree branches; I came out and beat the animal with it from left to right and from left and right again and again until I had no more reason to be angry anymore.

But then, "What do I do now?" I thought. "How on earth am I going to get close enough to the donkey to load it with those bundles?" I said aloud. Outside of the house there was a section of a high wood fence separating the property from the main road and it seemed to be the only solution to my problem, at least for now. I untied the halter from the door handle and passed it through the fence. From the roadside, I pulled the donkey's head close to the fence, about three inches and then I tied the rope to a nearby pole so the animal could not turn its head and see what I was up to. I walked back to the house and retrieved the two bundles of branches which I secured onto the donkey's back, keeping as far as I could away from its behind.

When I finished, I walked around the fence again and untied the rope which I passed through the fence, this time with the help of a stick. I picked up the end of the halter in front of the farmhouse, I pulled it and came back home walking and running at the same time, making sure there was enough space between us. I told my uncle what had happened and he said he wasn't surprised at all.

A friend of my uncle told me later that the donkey had tried to attack my uncle from behind and a couple of times bit his right shoulder. Eventually my uncle feared for his own life and got rid of the animal as soon as he could.

I spent most of my teenage years in school and helping my father either in distributing some mail or playing the organ in church whenever he had other things to do; but I never had the luxury of extra money in my pocket and neither did my friend Antonio. Our common friend Elio was the only one making some money as a helping hand in a blacksmith shop.

One beautiful day during the summer, Toni and I took a walk through the town's market place and saw some juicy green and black figs, but we had no money to buy them, so we walked back home very disappointed- The next day we discussed a very strange and peculiar plan to convince our friend Elio to buy those special figs.

Not too far from our homes, there is a zig-zag road that connects the lower part of Tagliacozzo, around the hill where we lived and finally leading to other towns in higher altitudes than ours, like Cappadocia. This beautiful winding road adorned with magnificent pine trees is a haven for who wants to take a short walk especially during the long summer evenings. We decided to change all that by creating a nonsense nightmare for everybody.

Here is what we did: we gave my brother Luigi a white bed sheet and made him hide behind the wall of the last building on that road, just before the pine trees area. At a given signal he would come out, wrapped in that sheet and dance in the middle of the road.

Around 9 p.m. Toni and I knocked at Elio's front door and his mother opened it and made us go in. Elio was about to finish his supper. Then we asked him to go out with us for a walk. At first, he said he was very tired but we finally convinced him anyway. We started to walk down toward that last house and to our amusement nobody was anywhere around the whole area that night.

A few steps into the trees, I said, "We better go back!" "What?" Elio asked. "I want to go back, too!" said Toni. "But why?" Elio demanded. I finally said, "I heard that somebody had seen a white ghost dancing in the middle of the road, right at this spot!"

"And you still believe those nonsense stories?" Elio answered. "It is true!" I said, and as I turned I gave Luigi the signal by rubbing my sneakers hard into the ground. Luigi came out of his hiding place and started to dance in the middle of the road. Terrified, we ran in the opposite direction as fast as we could. Elio was really scared and holding a pocket knife. He was talking to himself. Toni and I were more scared just by looking at him.

Naturally we couldn't come back the same way, so we walked a sort of semi-circle and came back by passing through the market plaza where the woman selling the magnificent figs was. Elio bought a few pounds of figs which we ate on our way back up our homes. Just the way we had planned.

The news about that ghost became the talk of the town and not too many people ventured down that road at night for a while. Toni and I felt really deep remorse for what we had done and could not hold that secret too long. When we found enough courage to tell Elio the truth he was furious and he had all reason to be, but we felt really relieved. As I said before we were young and always looking for adventures of any kind.

Not long after my uncle sold his donkey, for no apparent reason he didn't come to see his mother anymore. A few times I saw him making long, unnecessary trips to avoid passing in front of our house. Don Gaetano found out and tried unsuccessfully to talk to my uncle and to my father, who by now wasn't talking to his brother either.

Any attempt seemed to fail until a week or two before Christmas. My father was having a drink with one of his friends and my uncle passed by. My father's friend knew him from way back in the United States, invited my uncle to join in for a drink. On that occasion, my father made peace with his brother. They talked and drank at the same time and when they felt very happy under the influence of the alcohol, of course, arm in arm they walked back home and my uncle stopped to see my grandmother.

I never forgot that scene. My grandmother was in bed with injuries to her leg after a fall in front of the house. On both ends of that antique bed, there were two very high iron poles ending with two decorated knobs. My uncle grabbed one pole and my father the other. They both laughed, sang and looked at their mother who, waving her finger at them and reprimanded them as if they were four or five years old. We all were happy for that, and Don Gaetano attributed that small miracle to incessant prayers.

I have good memories of my school years in Avezzano, despite the experience with that professor Nardelli about the Foffano deal as I mentioned before. We had a very talented music teacher: Prof. Galeone. He was very small in stature, and unfortunately, we students took advantage of him. We used to ridicule and tease him. He could hardly reach the top of the blackboard and every time he drew a music staff, we accompanied his hand with a lot of Booooo! and Oooooo! Sometimes he turned his head fast but never caught anybody.

Other times we wore small miniature bells under our pants and played them from opposite sides of the classroom. We loved to see him running from one end of the room to the other and never catch anyone. After a while we all got tired of that nonsense attitude and started to listen to him playing the piano instead. He played it very well, despite the small size of his hands; he reached all the keys mostly with each side of his fingers, in an arpeggio manner.

Sometimes he told us about his life experiences. He had written an opera called *Clarissa*. Financially he could not present it to the public. He met and married a wealthy woman who helped him put up that opera in one of Italy's well-known theaters, and the event seemed to be great.

There was only one thing wrong. He directed and also

conducted the orchestra and that was a big mistake. His poor personality tragically affected the imposition and the seriousness of the drama the opera represented. Not only the spectators felt disappointment, but the press treated him very rudely. That was the end of the opera, and also the end of the teacher's marriage. We all felt very bad for him. He did play for us some of the opera's themes and we all thought that was beautiful music. Too bad!

After my college graduation, right in the middle of WWII, I had a job in our town's city hall. One of my responsibilities was to provide all kinds of documents that people requested daily at our teller's window. When a few bombs were dropped in the San Lorenzo area in Rome, a few young wives of military personnel evacuated that zone and took refuge in our town. Our office's duty was to help process the transfer of their monthly war checks.

One day two young women with children showed up at my window and asked to apply for those payment transfers and handed me their original payments books. When I looked at the books, I couldn't help laughing and that irritated the two ladies. They were two sisters married to two brothers whose last name was: Muori (dying). One of the sister's first name was Crocefissa (crucified), and the other, Consolata (consoled). They had their reasons to get upset and should have expected hilarious reactions after all.

The office of the mayor had the power to authorize monthly payments to needy people and acted according to the opinions of a commission in which the mayor himself, the police marshal, and two men from different part of the town participated. I was the secretary of that commission, and had the painful duty to relate the decision of each meeting to the people via the teller window. To my disappointment some of those decisions were unfair. A few times I was reprimanded by the police marshal for revealing the names of the members of the commission.

At the beginning of 1944, the Italian government issued a ministerial decree by which any widow who had only one son currently in the war, could request his discharge so he could come home and work at his own farm, provided that the family could prove the possession of a certain amount of land. There was a special form to fill out. It didn't take long for all the widows in town and from the nine villages under our jurisdiction, to come to our building the same day and about the same time.

I was in my office with my two office mates when two women walked in and asked us to please help them to fill out that petition. Reluctantly we did help and told them not to say anything to anyone because we had our own work to do. To our awful surprise, not even a half hour later our office looked like pandemonium. It became so crowded that our desks were pushed against the opposite wall and we got packed like sandwiches.

I couldn't help but get really upset and force all those women out of my office. While they were leaving more or less unwillingly, I noticed that one of my aunts on my father's side was in that group. "Oh no! What did I do now?" I asked myself. As soon as I closed the office, I stopped at her house in my way home and apologized the best I could for what I had done, promising to fill out that blessed application now.

She didn't want to hear any excuse about it. She thought that what I had done was done intentionally and not to bother her any longer. I felt very bad about it, but was more disappointed by that awful reaction. That misunderstanding didn't clarify until many years later during my visit back home from the United States. She told me she had created a nightmare for herself by acting the way she did.

Our town had a shooting range not too far from the main square and it was very active especially during the summer. The German SS used that range to execute two young boys from Rome's vicinity for espionage. Very early, on the day of the execution, a local farmer on his way to work saw the whole macabre operation and later related in detail all he had seen.

Father Lucidi, our local pastor, heard the boys' confessions and gave them their last rites. One of the

German officers gave the Italian police marshal the order to shoot. The marshal gave his own order to his subordinate police officers. And that was it! The poor man was still shaking while describing the scene.

After the shooting, the Italian marshal patted the German officer on the shoulder and said, "We did justice!" He remained in office till the end of the war, then he disappeared. The whole town forgave the marshal the duties of his unpleasant job; he had a big family to support. But his evil remark was never forgiven. We also found out that those boys were innocent of any wrong-doing, and that made the matter worse.

By a very strange fate, that marshal had loaned some money to a local lady and came back for it. Although he no longer wore the police uniform, he was soon recognized and before long a lot of people assembled outside that lady's house, including myself! We all forced him out of the house and dragged him to the shooting range and for sure it looked like it was the end of him by general angry consent.

Fortunately, the town was getting ready for the election of the first free democratic vote for the mayor and a very bright young lawyer (Paoluzi) was running for it. We all had great esteem for him and trusted his ability to control the confusion left after a very long war. He stopped that angry crowd on time, and used his well-put strategy to convince everybody of the right way to process the marshal.

It took a few hours to disperse all the people after the marshal was taken to the city hall building, but thank God, the future mayor was able to avoid a very regrettable action from our part. The marshal was later processed and wound up in jail.

As soon as the railroad was repaired, we were able to travel in wagons used to transport livestock. Each one of those wagons had a big steel sliding door that most of the time was open. A long iron bar, from one side of the door to the other, served as a window sill and we could rest our arms on it, while looking at the quickly changing green panorama during our daily trips to the near town of Avezzano.

In the summer and the first part of the fall, it was a pleasure to ride in that fashion but when the winter came it was another matter. On one of those winter mornings, I was riding that train with a couple of school mates and with my friend Vinicio's father, Vincenzo. It was very cold, so all four of us tried to close that blessed door, but could not move it. We all rested our elbows on the bar and talked about the weather, while the train was going at a moderate speed. I was standing on the beginning of the sliding door track and Vincenzo was at the end.

Just before the railroad station, the train put on the

breaks slowly and to my horror I saw the door take off with violence. The two other passengers and I got out the way screaming, but not Vincenzo. The door crushed him so badly against the door frame, he was all black and blue. He was rushed to the Avezzano hospital; they could not do too much for him. He died a few days later. What a shame!

At the end of 1946 and the beginning of 1947 we were able to ride the first post-war passenger train. I remember applying for a daily railroad pass to Aielli, further east of Avezzano. A priest friend of Don Gaetano, allowed me to practice on a beautiful organ in that town's main church. A beautiful experience!

I also traveled to Scurcola Marsicana by train and played the organ there for a Schola cantorum. The railroad station is more than a mile away from the church and my timing sometimes was critical. One rainy day, I came running while the train was leaving. I stepped with my left foot on the step of the moving train while trying to get hold of the door handle with my left hand. My foot slid and fortunately my pants caught the edge of the step until I secured my right foot on it. What a relief!

On one of the trips I took to Rome, mostly for school purposes, my name made the headline in the national daily newspaper, Il Messaggero. I was getting off the train about five p.m. and saw some of my friends looking at me somewhat surprised. "What happened Peppino?" they asked. "What?" I said. "According to the newspaper, you are supposed to be in jail—look!" one of them said, handing me the paper, and there it was. My name in bold letters, right on the front page.

Somebody with my name had killed a young girl in front of St. John's Basilica in Rome early in the morning, about the time I had just arrived in Roma Termini. So I kept the town in turmoil all day for a change, but, thank God, I missed a horrifying story.

One of my college friends, Pietro Di Rocco, knew of my frequent trips to Rome and one day he asked me to do him a favor. He had a five hundred lire bill and nobody in town would cash it. Would I be able to stop at the treasury building in Rome and find out what to do with it? "No problem!" I said. I took that bill with me and on my next trip to the big city I showed it to one of the window clerks in the treasury department.

In a matter of few minutes, two agents were at my side and asked me to follow them to one of the investigators' offices. For about two hours they asked me all kinds of questions such as my address, my friends, my family, my daily activities, etc. That bill was one of a falsified money series for which the police were investigating the source. I related that unpleasant news to my friend who apologized for the trouble he had caused after I had told him I was very upset about the whole thing.

About a year later, during a week-long religious feast in town, I came across the police marshal I knew very well and in confidence he told me that for a year he had followed me wherever I went. They finally caught up with the gang responsible for the false money, but I felt more uncomfortable than the previous year, just knowing that I had been watched so often, and by the police on top of it all!

While working in Tagliacozzo's city hall, I held two consecutive part-time jobs. One concerned paper work dealing with war related matters such as agriculture assistance and regulations; it was discontinued in 1945. The other was in the registration office and was given back to the original clerks that came home from military duties.

As soon as I left, a young man about my age who had a steady position in the same office, died of a heart attack. I went to visit with some friends and I felt very disturbed when one of the young man's relatives, looking towards us angrily, said, "Somebody will be happy to get his job!" A few days later the mayor sent for me about the job but I refused it. At the beginning of 1947 I was offered a teaching job in a faraway village, for little money. I would have had to go on foot and it was not worth the shoes' value.

CHAPTER SEVEN

My Recollection of 1944

With the exception of a few trips to the drug store, the doctor, food shopping, the bank or occasional activities at our club house such as games of bocce, billiards or table tennis, I spend a good part of my retirement day-dreaming, sitting in my favorite chair, which I mentioned earlier. I shift positions now and then, and as soon as my body is comfortable, my mind takes me on those magical trips to the past. Fantasy is a beautiful pastime, especially when you think of a dear friend or relative whose names are very familiar, and you want to remember exactly the way they looked or talked, and that takes time. But it is time well spent. The same applies to facts and circumstances which are not so pleasant and that may be a reason why we remember them better, such as war time. What about the war? What about my 1944?

We were living under a totalitarian government and

for that reason we were not aware of the true political situation world-wide. During the winter of 1943, we didn't even know who our military friends were. Our government fell and confusion spread all over Italy. The Germans, once our allies, literally took over all of our land. We felt a shortage of food and other necessities. Very often we were lucky to find an egg or a half pound of dirty black salt in exchange for a good piece of land.

I had just graduated from college, but temporarily out of work because of the war under way. All my friends from school or from my neighborhood were in the army, and at the moment may be missing in action or prisoners of either the Americans or the Germans. Early in May 1944, all the schools closed in a hurry. We found out that the Germans occupied mid-north Italy, through mural posters all over the walls of the town's buildings, written in three languages: Italian, German and English.

The Italian soil was now under German dominion. We were told to be calm and please leave all telephone and telegraph lines alone and categorically keep out of the German military operations. If by any chance we would cause any damage to the soldiers, they would retaliate by taking as many as thirty hostages and probably killing them, for every German soldier either wounded or killed.

Steady air raids and occasional bombings from either the Germans or Allied forces were the order of most days. Young mothers didn't know where to run for cover to protect their children. A pitiful sight!

Luckily, I had found temporary work as a clerk in the local municipal building, but the Germans too often made unexpected visits looking for men to do their war projects—naturally most of the young men were at war —so they often took us clerks to either shovel snow, dig ground for anti air strike shelters, or go to the concentration camps. Not a very pleasant choice.

Occasionally I thought I could have been better off in the army where the enemy was only on one side of you; here at home all of us, young and old alike, could be destroyed from anywhere, any time of the day or night. Through the underground radio we found out that the allied forces, after the bitter resistance of Monte Cassino, were now on their way to the Abruzzo region. We were confident that in matter of days our situation would change, and that gave us all courage to endure our miseries for the moment.

We all were given food certificates for 200 grams of what looked like bread on the outside, but inside was a mixture of dirty wheat and pieces of cement rocks. It was bad but better than nothing at all. Fortunately, that food shortage only lasted a few months.

A few times, coming home I found my stepmother Zia Concetta crying over the food not being enough for all of us. I had a hard time convincing her to take care of Maria and Domenico who needed more protection than myself and Luigi, who were already grown up. It really looked bad but not enough to break my faith and confidence. I was sure God was with us always.

Food came strangely unexpectedly and I would say miraculously. How could I otherwise explain a strange circumstance in which a family friend, Toto Troini, who was a local merchant, whom we didn't see for about a year and as far as I could remember never came to our home, came unexpectedly to visit during this period and gave Zia Concetta two pounds of rice? That particular day she didn't have a thing for us to eat at all.

On another occasion, my father's sister (Teresina) who lived in the village of Poggetello, about two miles away, let my father know that she had some small potatoes, the kind which normally were given to the pigs. If we wanted them, don't hesitate to come get them. Why not?

I didn't waste any time, I walked my way through farms because the main road was in continuous danger of possible air strikes. On my way back, about halfway home, I met a friendly farmer who was going my way with his well loaded donkey. He made me put my bundle of potatoes on the animal's back and we slowly headed home.

We were about to cross the Rome-Pescara railroad, near the cemetery when suddenly, a bombers squad appeared from out of nowhere in the skies. The donkey, even though the farmer pulled violently by his heavy strap and I whipped him from behind, stood tragically still. We finally gave up and made it just on time to fall into a ditch by the road side.

A few minutes later, a bomb exploded not too far from where we were, creating an enormous hole in the ground. We saw pieces of metal and rocks flying above our heads and then heard a terrible silence. We came out of our improvised shelter and started to laugh like two little boys; we saw the donkey had left the railroad crossing in a hurry and was now waiting for us a few hundred feet away. Those little potatoes that I was finally able to take home that day, seemed to have a special flavor.

During this period, almost every day, a siren, which was installed in the church of Annunziata's bell tower, put the whole town under an air raid warning for more than two hours. That sound, somewhat terrifying, caused real panic especially for all the women with their children. We used to remain in apprehension, waiting for unknown terror. We often took improvised shelters, lacking real safety; just like when we were young, running frightened under the bed. We were adapting ourselves to a new, strange life routine. What else could we do?

I wasn't too enthusiastic to be home while all my friends were in various war grounds. As a matter of fact, I felt uneasy and uncomfortable for not being able to participate in military duties. I used to be embarrassed just walking by the houses where the mothers of my friends who were prisoners or missing-in-action lived—especially when I heard them sobbing. Most of the time I preferred making useless trips through the countryside just to avoid seeing those poor women to whom I resembled their own sons.

As a matter of routine, our small group of city clerks and older men that happened to be home at that time became a bunch of improvised miners; digging holes or trenches for shelters and anti-air strikes. One day, I left the office to go to lunch and sure enough one soldier tried to get my attention by yelling German phrases behind me. I tried to ignore him but, looking up ahead, I saw a lady from her kitchen window pleading with me to turn around. The soldier was about to shoot me. I stood there, death frozen, for few minutes.

One day I was home eating my make-believe bread and a neighbor woman walked in looking at me and said, "Are you eating that garbage?" "I have no alternative!" I answered. "Please give me a piece, I want to show it to my son who is driving me nuts!" she added. He would complain about the food that was available to the public at that time. From then on, he didn't complain any more. A couple of days after, a German officer needed some men to do some work out in the field and took me and that lady's son as well.

We left very early in the morning and I took my portion of 200 grams of bread for my lunch. My friend ate his portion on our way to the place. At noon, we took some time off for lunch and sat on the ground. My friend had nothing to eat and asked me if I had ever eaten hot peppers. I said: "No!" He said: "Strange! I am very surprised! You are really missing good stuff. Try and see for yourself!" I gave him my bread and he took out a red hot pepper and spread it on it. He gave me the bread back and as soon as I put it close to my mouth I saw stars. A very clever trick! He ate his bread and mine after all.

I remember Joseph, a German officer, very well. Every morning, he showed us where we had to prepare the holes in the rock to be removed by the mines; later he came back and loaded the mines and made them explode. We were working on an anti-air shelter, shaped like an underground tunnel where two teams of men came in from opposite directions and eventually would meet in the center.

The day the two teams met, Joseph gave a party and brought in a bottle of Strega liquor for the occasion. That particular day I was sick in bed with fever. When the bottle was about to be finished, Joseph said that that portion was for me, the other Joseph, and told everybody to come to see me. That happy party continued in my house and Joseph seemed to be so happy; he sang and danced with my grandmother Maria. He also showed us, with pride, the picture of his wife and a young son in front of his house in Germany.

A few days later, Joseph took his own life with his

pistol while driving his jeep along one of the main roads in downtown Tagliacozzo. In one hand he had a letter from his commander, telling him that his wife and son had died a few days earlier as a result of a bitter air strike that had destroyed his house also.

The town of Tagliacozzo sits between two high mountains; on the peak of the left mountain (north), there is a huge high iron cross, erected by missionaries in 1930, while on the peak of the right one (south), there was up to that time, a big metal Fascio (Fascist emblem), erected by the Fascist party in 1922 and demolished at the end of the current conflict.

Directly below the cross, the German soldiers had discovered a large cave, accessible by a narrow road coming from the church of Madonna del Soccorso (the highest part of town). A few times, we had to clear that road and also remove rocks or dirt from the cave. In my quick visits to that cave I took a fast look around and I noticed plenty of ammunition, jeeps and small trucks.

One day, while working on this side, after the usual terrifying sound of the siren, I noticed an American plane dropping two bombs. I couldn't run anywhere, so I laid down burying my head in the grass. I waited a few seconds and then I looked again. They looked like two pills coming directly at me. A few moments after I heard a big explosion and saw a big black cloud about a couple miles away, not too far from the railroad station.

"Oh my God!" I said to myself, remembering that my brother Luigi, also working with other German soldiers, was right there that day. Luckily, he was working below the ground level in an improvised cemetery for all the dead German coming from the Monte Cassino resistance. He had been very scared but physically unharmed. I imagine that the Americans knew exactly where General Rommel's temporary headquarters were at that time; in an isolated villa, very close to where those explosions occurred.

Early in the morning of an unforgettable day, June 6, 1944, I had left my house to go to our little vineyard in Casalone, about a mile away, and spray the grape plants with a chemical substance diluted in water to destroy the parasites visible on the leaves. In order to do that, I wore a special pump strapped to my shoulders, with the spraying hose in my left hand and the pressure handle in my right.

It's a job that usually takes between two to three hours to do. This was the second time my father let me do that job and I was proud to assume a little responsibility in the household's adult chores. My father was very busy as the only mail carrier in town, besides the necessary domestic routines.

That same morning, my father had left home carrying a bundle of thin poles to be used for the tomato plants we had in a small garden near the railroad. He told me that he was going to leave those poles in a trench near the post office and retrieve them in the afternoon after work. He also said that he hoped to be home sometimes before dark, after he had planted those blessed poles.

I finished my job and headed home at about two p.m. I ate something in the kitchen and then went out and sat, relaxing a little on the front step of my house. All of sudden, a group of about twenty men coming from the low part of town—screaming and waving all kind of wooden and iron clubs—were running toward the Soccorso, the high part of town. One of them stopped in front of me and in a somewhat sarcastic voice said, "Look at you! Aren't you ashamed? So very relaxed, while your father is in a puddle of blood?" "Where?" I asked desperately. "In one of those buildings behind the Obelisco square!" They all answered, while running the opposite way. "Cowards!" I thought right then and there.

Zia Concetta, my stepmother, suspecting something serious, came running down the steps, crying. I tried to calm her down and immediately ran toward those buildings. I found a few women gathered in front of the Bonaventura's palace and they pointed to the door leading to the basement. There I found my father, all alone, sitting on the last stairway step of the very dark cellar. He was crying and desperately holding his left leg which was bleeding very badly from the knee. In between sobs, he mumbled incoherent phrases and asked to be forgiven for what had happened.

I was moved and mad at the same moment, but could not waste any more time and definitely could not do much by myself. I went out of the building and frantically screamed for help. Thank God, a few men ran up and in no time, we were able to take my father to the local hospital. A bullet had passed from one side of his left knee to the other. After the first round of emergency medications, I stayed a while with my father, who by now was frightened and shaking, probably more aware of the damage he had done to himself and the rest of his family than anything else.

What had happened? My father didn't have the courage to tell me, but one of the men who had helped me to take him to the hospital told me about it. According to the latest development, we had suspected a possible retreat of the German troops toward north Italy, after the loss of Monte Cassino, and the few soldiers who strolled about town, probably members of the demolition squad, would have orders to demolish not only the railroad tracks but also the little hydroelectric cabin we had in the Capacqua location.

A few men, my father included and without my knowledge, had discussed that matter earlier and decided that whoever suspected that unacceptable project, would run to the bell tower of St. Francis' church and ring one of the bells. That would be the signal for all the other men to run toward the electric cabin armed with either clubs, rocks or pieces of wood, to try to stop the German soldiers from demolishing the cabin.

When the bell rang, my father was on his way to the garden with that bundle of poles. At once he dropped that bundle by the roadside and while running toward the cabin, he came across two German soldiers who at the moment gave up their project to take away a hostage, someone my father knew very well. Acting as a new patriotic hero, my father picked up a stone and threw it at one of the soldiers who turned and pulled his gun out and shot my father point blank at his left leg, probably to scare him. In conclusion, the cabin was demolished awhile later. When the two officers joined the rest of the demolition crew coming from Monte Cassino, that man was released and my father got his foolish reward.

In the hospital bed next to my father, there was a middle-aged man in a very pitiful shape. A nun told me that he was an ex-allied prisoner of war. I took a closer look at him and recognized him instantly. The poor man had run away from a prisoners' camp nine months earlier and my uncle, Quirino Di Giampaolo from Poggetello, found him in a thick wooded area near his farm, close to the village. My uncle gave him food and clothes to face the inconveniences of the moment, but most of all to prevent him from being captured again.

A few times, my uncle sent me to feed him; he made me put on my clothes inside-out and wear funny hats for precaution. On one of those trips, I saw the man's face, and that's why I recognized him at the hospital. By a bizarre fate, he became seriously ill at the last minute, just before the allied liberation. He died the next day, June 7, a few hours before the first American truck entered our town. A crude coincidence!

As soon as my father calmed down a little, I went back home just before dark and curfew time. I told my stepmother every detail. She started to cry, but not for long for fear of upsetting the children. My brother Luigi was uneasy and strangely nervous. We all went to bed to try to rest and save some energy which we would need to face the uncertain tomorrow; not too pleasant for sure.

The morning of June 7, after a night often disturbed by sporadic gunshots, didn't promise much. I knew I had left my father at the hospital the night before in a worried state. I decided to go visit him, no matter what. My stepmother, Zia Concetta, gave me two eggs for my father and warned me to be careful.

As I stepped out the house, I met six friends of mine and a young lady I knew, Antonina. They were carrying a small wooden ladder as an improvised stretcher on which they had placed a seriously wounded man. His name was Gaetano, Antonina's boyfriend, an Italian ex-army officer. They were in a hurry to the hospital. As a funny coincidence, that company served my purpose as well.

While we passed the bridge over the railroad near the hospital, we met a woman, Fernanda, in visible shock. She was pointing her finger to the body of her father, killed by the Germans earlier. Evidently, the poor man, came out of the house holding a sickle with the intention of working on his garden, but the German soldiers must have considered him too dangerous and fired at him, killing him. We couldn't stop for long because we wanted to get to the hospital as soon as we could and to try to save the Italian officer's life.

At the hospital, the doctor in charge removed the young officer's shirt and we saw a small blood spot on his chest, but on his back, where the bullet had exploded coming out, there was a big cavity from which the blood was coming out profusely. We all looked at the doctor who gave us a discouraging expression on his face and at the same time Antonina fainted. I gave the nurse one of the two eggs to give to the girl when she would come around and I left the room to go see my father who was much calmer and less frightened than the previous evening.

His leg was well-positioned over a cushion;. For a second I didn't think his leg could be saved. I gave him the other egg and I left in a hurry because I wanted to go back home in the company of the same group of friends, just for protection. You could tell something was terribly wrong in the air that day. The American prisoner and the young Italian officer died a little while later.

As we were near our homes, in the Fuori Porta locality, we came across an S.S. German Officer and four other soldiers armed with machine guns, pistols, and hand grenades ready to use. They ordered us to stop and after they looked at that ladder covered with blood stained sheets and blankets, they accused all of us of being part of a sabotage group that had damaged their trucks and had stolen some machine guns the night before. We were order to line up by the curb of the main road with our hands above our heads; they categorically prohibited us to turn around for any reason at all. They didn't even bother looking at our I.D. cards that we had taken out our pockets.

After about half an hour in that uncomfortable position and listening to an animated discussion those soldiers had behind our back, a lady from the window across the street, Annina, saw that somewhat dubious scene and started to scream. All of sudden we heard a gunshot and the first young man on the left of the lineup fell to the ground, unconscious. I was the last one on the right and the fellow next to me, Giacomo Cellini, panicked and asked me what to do. While I was telling him to say a prayer, I saw his black beard instantly change to white.

He thought that the soldiers were killing us all, starting from the left side; but his nephew Nando, the first man on the left, thought the opposite and had fainted from fear. What really happened was that the German Officer had fired his gun up in the air to intimidate the screaming woman. A few minutes later, another German officer came around on his motorcycle and gave orders for us to go free.

At home, everybody and everything was fine. I told Zia Concetta the story, ate something and then went to see my friends a couple doors away. I sat by the fire place and started to tell them what had happened that morning. Suddenly the front door was forced open and an S.S. officer, with the unmistakable threatening miter ordered me and my two friends Mario and Antonio to go out in the street.

While standing there, we saw another armed officer go into my house. Luckily, my brother Luigi made it on time to lock himself out onto the bedroom balcony; the door is somewhat disguised and not too easy to find. The soldier came out empty handed from my house but found a middle age man, Vincenzo Rampa in the next house. The first officer ordered all four of us to walk in the direction of Poggiogalle's semi-isolated three-story house in a less populated area, Fuori Porta, where the Germans had an improvised general military command.

An older man, Bettino Santariga, was resting in front of his house not too far from there. He had just gotten home from an exhausting trip to the mountains. The same German officer ordered him to join us and arrogantly led us to the third floor of Poggiogalle house and made sure we were locked in. It was now about one in the afternoon, and after about ten minutes, the rough-looking commander came up. We listened to all the insults and accusations; he also mentioned the theft of ammunitions from one of their trucks and finally, always in German, he said that we would be executed at 9 p.m. He showed us the number with his fingers and to be sure we understood him, he took some gun bullets from his pockets and called them "confetti" for the ceremony.

We now realized the macabre situation we were in. We had heard stories about other hostages taken in other parts of our region being executed, always five in the group. I'll try to describe the best I can all the impressions and reactions in the minds of all of us condemned to die. In reality, they are masterpieces of humorist chronicles.

Our improvised prison had a wooden chest against one of the walls. The two older men, Bettino Santariga and Vincenzo Rampa, were sitting on it, while Mario Onofri, Antonio Verna and myself sat on a bed's box spring, on the adjoining wall.

As soon as the commander left, Mario stared to cry convulsively, while Antonio got up and walked around the room, testing all the walls for a weak spot—but the only window we had was right above the main entrance to the building, now guarded by so many armed soldiers. From that window, I could see my brother over the hill across way; he was crying. We also noticed some squirrels running around the woods and ironically, they seemed to have more right to live than us human beings. However, I was able to say some prayers.

Bettino was telling his friend that if anything would happened to him, he felt sorry for his wife who was not so clever in handling their children. Every morning she hesitates in waking them up to go to work and that would surely create a shortage of food for the whole family, especially during the current world conflict. Vincenzo said that he had a better reason to worry, since he had hidden some money without his wife's knowledge. Clown's stuff!

The news about our capture traveled fast all over the town and some women relatives were allowed to come up and visit us. They brought in food and wine with the intention of calming down the German officers who didn't even look at those bags. The ladies were a little upset at first, but when we mentioned the death threat, a pandemonium exploded like a bomb or something; their screams could be heard a kilometer away. Two of them went around town pleading with the people for the restitution of that blessed ammunition as soon as possible.

I found out later that my stepmother, Zia Concetta went into St. Peter's church and while some people were praying, she put my little brother Domenico on the altar to Our Lady of Grace and offered him to God in exchange for my life. An astonishing statement that is in my heart for as long as I live!

During that confusion, someone thought of locating a man by the name of Eugenio Baiocco, who understood German a little and pleaded with him to talk to the German commander who naturally didn't pay any attention to what the man was saying. At this time, Don Gaetano Tantalo, our pastor, conscious of the situation, came in and pleaded with the German officer to take him in exchange for us five. At first, the officer tried to dissuade him, but when the priest insisted, he made him come up and keep us company.

Don Gaetano, although deeply worried about the fate of a Jewish family under his protection at the moment, came in, always smiling, and assured us that Our Lady would certainly come to our rescue if we prayed sincerely and constantly. I doubted my friends believed in what Don Gaetano was saying, but I was convinced, since I knew by now, that he knew exactly what would be the outcome. A few years earlier, while I was a member of a young Catholic group, I reprimanded a group of young girls for reading a magazine, at that time not likely approved by our catechism class standards. On my way home I met Don Gaetano, who praised me for no apparent reason. After that day, I suspected his supernatural gift. I got evident proof a couple of years later when he passed away.

About half hour after Don Gaetano had come in, the

commander came up and seeing us on our knees, praying, he seemed visibly changed. Besides the rosary, always wrapped around his right hand, Don Gaetano also had a book about the contemporary war situation. I remember very well the cover of that book. It was diagonally divided into two parts, representing Italian and German troops with the respective pictures of Mussolini and Hitler. The officer smiled while looking at us and the book. He offered us some cigarettes. We offered him some wine that he drank only after he made us drink it first.

He left the room and returned a few minutes later. This time, to our unexpected surprise, he said that he would release all of us, with the promise that two of the hostages would help his soldiers to install some telephone wires in a different part of town. The two older men and Mario were released at about 5 p.m. Antonio and I, wearing special telephone equipment on our shoulders, had to follow some soldiers toward the piazza which is in the lower part of our town.

Naturally we were very happy to be free in a way, but constantly in danger all night long because we didn't wear military uniforms and naturally were an easy target for all the soldiers circulating in the zone. Thank God, the men in our crew, prevented the surely deadly shooting just in time.

We finished that work around midnight and were taken to the main floor of a private house, ready to be released. Instead, either satisfied for a job well done, or discouraged about the imminent end of the Nazi era, they started to abuse alcohol and use insults and threats of every kind towards us. This senseless joke lasted a couple of hours, until an officer came in and took us uptown in his jeep.

I finally got home at two in the morning and found Zia Concetta, my brother Luigi and my grandmother Maria waiting in the kitchen, lighted by the last centimeter of a candle. (We had no electricity from the previous night.) We all rejoiced over the happy end of a really bad day. I, for my part, attributed everything to my faith, which in this case assumed a new meaning: miracle! Soon we joined the two children already asleep.

Very early the next day, expecting unknown developments of the situation in general, I took my brother Luigi with me to the church of St. Anthony which I mentioned before, and I made him hide on the main altar behind a huge wooden statue of the saint and told him not to move for any reason. I settled in the sacristy, by the window facing the southeast part of the city, where we were expecting anything to happen at any moment.

A couple of hours later, I saw the railroad being destroyed, a fraction at a time, every few minutes. At noon, a man by the name of Francesco Simone came up a long ladder which rested below the little window where I was, and with plenty of paint and a brush replaced the big word "DUCE", clearly visible from the railroad station with a much better word "LIBERTA'". That was the first positive sign of the end of the Fascist and Nazi odyssey and at least the end of the one big problem. Other lesser problems were approaching.

Around midday, Luigi and I came out of our hiding place, a little over-elated, just thinking about the imminent end of those awful hostilities. In the afternoon we saw the first New Zealand trucks, part of the alley convoy enter our town, coming from the south. All the civilians joined them in a long overdue celebration that lasted a few days. At least one problem seemed solved.

During the week my father came home and a neighbor lady, Assunta Onofri, assumed the duty of an improvised nurse by forcing a piece of sterilized gauze from one side of my father's knee and retrieving it out the other side of the perforation, causing indescribable pain for the poor man. In spite of what seemed like the proper precaution, a bad infection stepped in, producing a progressive swelling in the whole leg. Evidently the bullet that hit my father had been immersed in some poisoned solution for disastrous purpose.

After three weeks, we were doubtful of the possibility of saving my father's leg, because all the facilities in the main cities in the Abruzzo region were isolated. The railroad was completely destroyed and the main highways were either badly damaged or scattered with dangerous mines. It was impossible to go anywhere even though a lot of people were willing to help. Unfortunately, what was lacking were specific directives from a well-organized command.

We were at the mercy of bad outbursts of oppressed personal resentments, causing confusion of new political parties fully opposing one another, worse than real enemies in the battlefield. Surviving soldiers who, little by little, came home from opposite war fronts, very often quarreled in the streets and sometimes used their hands. In many cases it was a pitiful situation to see two or more brothers insulting each other in the presence of their mother who, with tears and despair in her eyes, feared for their safety.

About the end of July, my father's leg was so swollen that he had to keep the good leg out of the bed for lack of space. God again took over the situation. An American jeep came to a sudden stop right in front of my house and Zia Concetta's brother, Vincenzo, who was declared missing in action, a couple of years earlier, came out of the passenger's side. His sister thought he was dead.

We could not believe our eyes. He had been held prisoner near Yugoslavia, and when he found out that the American forces had reached Monte Cassino, he escaped with some of his friends by boat to the Italian coast and joined an American group as a helping hand in their kitchen, until the front passed our zone over

Rome. One of his friends, an Italo-American sergeant, volunteered to take him to my house by jeep.

I will never forget the amount of food, clothing and medicine we received that day. When the sergeant saw my father in that pitiful condition, he volunteered to take him to the hospital in Rome immediately, in spite of the risks of mines. That same afternoon, we placed my father in the jeep; the big toe of his bad leg was inches away from the steering wheel. I could only imagine how difficult driving could be, mostly through wooded areas to avoid mine fields and at the same time not to disturb my father who was already in so much pain.

It took us about 3 hours to travel the 50 miles, but my father checked in at the Policlinico hospital in Rome and was placed in the only stretcher in the street level hallway, in the absence of a room and bed. A lot of casualties had occurred that day in Rome and the vicinity, therefore that big hospital was overcrowded. In the corridor I came across a male nurse from my hometown and he promised to find a bed for my father as soon as he could but discouraged me from trying to talk to the then top surgeon, Prof. Giangrasso.

My father's life was much more important than the nurse's warning and I decided to wait for the surgeon, outside the operating room. After about two hours, he came out and I gathered all my courage to describe the danger my father was facing. I will never forget the patience and the cordiality of that man; he promised to take care of my father as soon as he could. Zio Vincenzo took me to the apartment he was sharing with the Americans, within walking distance from the hospital, and as soon as I touched the bed I fell asleep instantly.

Early the next day in the hospital, I found out that my father had his own bed and at that time, 7:30 a.m., he was in the operating room. In the nearby waiting room, I found a middle-aged man crying over a boy's screams from the operating room. That poor man had just brought in his young boy who had picked up one of those miniature mines hidden in a toy that had exploded in the boy's hand and now he was wondering about the number of fingers the surgeon could save.

I tried my best to calm him down and while we were talking we heard a man screaming just as badly as the boy. I then made him realize that at least he knew that the problem with the boy was only the hand, while it could have been a matter of life or death for that older patient.

A little later I was allowed to go see my father in a huge room with about 40 beds, all occupied by men of all ages in a sitting position eating their breakfast; only one bed was covered with a white sheet from head to foot. I instantly realized that the man who was screaming earlier was my father, and I must have reacted very badly because one of the patients by the door made a sign for me to go over to him. He said,

"Don't get alarmed. Your father came in from the operating room a few minutes ago. He is now resting and the white sheet is protecting him from the bright light in the room."

The surgeon was able to save my father's leg by making incisions in different locations to stop the infection and swelling with no anesthesia whatsoever. I waited until he woke up. He told me he had suffered a lot but was now feeling better, at least morally, just thinking about being in a top hospital of the area. I spoke to Prof. Giangrasso about the sudden change of the beard color of my friend Cellini, on that infamous June 7, and he told me that it could have been possible.

That same day I left Rome and headed back to my town in Abruzzo the hard way; that is by hitchhiking, train, carriage, but mostly, by walking. I was able to get home by that night and give my family the good news. I felt very strong, and by now my faith was as solid as a rock.

Little by little things started to get better. My brother and I shared different chores, including distribution of some mail. The next few months I made trips to Rome, any way I could and quite often on foot. One particular day I rode a coal engine, wearing a white raincoat, and when I arrived at the hospital, I was welcomed with an unanimous laugh; I surely looked like a chimney sweeper!

By Christmas of 1944 my father came home with his

right leg stiff; he walked fairly well with the help of a cane. At the beginning of 1945, he resumed his normal service at the post office. My brother Luigi started to help my father with the mail and also with services in different churches as organist and custodian. In 1946 we were all happy that the war was over, but economically we were making very slow progress. In the fall of 1947, I planned to come to the United States where I emigrated in 1948.

With the help of my aunt Anna Maiolini, my father's sister, I started a new chapter of my life filled constantly with my unchanged faith. Finding work, making new friends, meeting my wife Rose, and raising a very nice family, were one continuous blessing after another. I am really content about my life so far. Thank GOD and my FAITH! I think I'll take another little nap right now!

PART THREE

MY NIGHTMARE, MY FUTURE

CHAPTER EIGHT

A Choice

It was 1947. The German troops who had taken over the Italian territory and part of Africa since 1943-1944 were retreating in a hurry either by sea at Anzio beach, near Rome, or by land beyond the Alps.

We had no idea of the actual international situation and had no news from our relatives overseas. All means of communications, even for a few miles, were disrupted. The railroad was destroyed completely by constantly exploding mines. All the highways were under continuous surveillance of bombers or light two-fuselage planes that could machine-gun at a short distance. I remember traveling to Rome by a bicycle with a friend and running under a heavy bridge during an unexpected air strike. We could hear the loud bomb explosion, followed by a heavy black smoke; an awful mixture of gravel and dirt that would settle back down in a matter of seconds. After that, a terrible silence.

During this time, which reminds me of the famous "Damocles' sword" which tells of the prospect of imminent danger, we received the first letter from my aunt, Zia Annina, in the USA written a year before. She was worried about all of us. I answered it at once; explaining our past odyssey, and at the same time reassured her of our present more comfortable situation. Just before Christmas of 1947, I received a letter saying there was a possibility of going to America after all. Someone would write and would give me all the information I needed.

Sure enough, I received another letter, from a man I did not know; he would meet me at a diner across from Genova's harbor, not too far from the railroad station. Naturally, in a small town like mine, it was very easy to create gossip and fantastic situations. People would have seen me at the local railroad station and that would have been sure proof of my sudden disappearance.

After quite a few hours on the train, I finally got off at the Genova station and walked into that blessed diner. A man approached me and said that, unfortunately it was impossible to take that trip for now. He apologized for the inconvenience and told me to be patient, go home and wait for the next opportunity. Naturally, all the townspeople were surprised when they saw me again walking around Tagliacozzo.

Right after Christmas, the man wrote me again and

guaranteed that everything was ready; he encouraged me to be strong and enthusiastic, and gave me an appointment at the same diner for January 31st at 8pm. This time I left my house as usual. Nobody paid me any attention. I took my raincoat and a little shopping bag with all my hygienic accessories and left. I went to the railroad station like I usually did when I would go to Rome.

On all those trips, I never met anybody from my hometown, but now further up in Genova there was only one person that I knew, and I met him as soon as I got off the train. It was a good thing he did not suspect anything.

At the diner, I put my bag down on the seat next to me and I ordered a coffee. A large clock was above the entrance door and I stared at it. It was a little after 8 pm so I decided to give up the idea altogether and picked up my bag and raincoat. All of a sudden, the man came in and looked at me, surprised. I didn't know what to say! I was rather confused, but again, he encouraged me and guaranteed that everything would be just right. He explained to me a strategic way to enter the ship, the Volcania.

I followed him a short distance and never took my eyes off of him. We walked for quite a while. He entered a lavatory that had two exit doors and as soon as I went in, he left me there and told me to lock both doors. I remained there for a long time and stared at both door handles that shook impatiently for the people who wanted to use the bathroom.

I then felt the movement of the ship as it left Genova and finally the man came back and we both came out of the lavatory. He took me to a room where there was a large closet. Inside there was another opening about 2 feet in circumference. I went into that slot and he sealed it with a piece of wood and white paint.

We then went to Naples, and after the ship stopped, I heard the constant noise of people and baggage in the nearby hallway. I couldn't sit. I was nervous, stiff as a board, and a little uncomfortable as far as breathing was concerned. I had no idea of the amount of time I remained in that miserable condition. Finally, I thought I felt the ship moving when that man came in and told me to come out of that trap. I discovered spots of paint on my raincoat. This time he took me to a lobby where there was a staircase to the second floor and locked both the entrance and exit doors.

With a screwdriver, he removed the front of the fifth step and let me get inside. In the scary complete darkness in the space under the staircase, I tried to mentally have an idea of the new residence, where I remained for the rest of my trip. I could finally sit down!

Since the man had closed the opening, I tried to get used to the darkness and very slowly I sorted out the contents of my shopping bag, as well as a commode and a urinal that the man had handed to me for my hygienic necessities. Even now I find it hard to believe how I could have had so much patience and moral readiness to bear such discomfort. Finally, I heard the ship move after a few days in that cavern, leaving Naples and headed to the USA.

After more than a week, the man came and locked both doors as usual. He removed the front of the fifth step and handed me a fireman's uniform and a flashlight. As soon as I put on that uniform, the man came and told me to come out of the hole. With the uniform on and having gained some weight, it was difficult. He pulled my arm very hard and I tried to twist myself the best I could. After a few minutes, I finally succeeded in getting out, but the sudden light made me faint. The man was losing his patience and told me it was time to leave the ship. Dressed as a fireman I would not be noticed as something abnormal. He also told me to walk ahead of him, not to turn around too often.

I kept on walking, walking toward the unknown. I came across an immense hall where there were a lot of people talking, laughing and screaming. I kept on walking and all of a sudden, I came across a man whose face I had seen in a lot of family pictures. My uncle, Zi'Ercole! My nightmare was over!

Part Four

End Notes

CHAPTER NINE
Don Gaetano, During 1944-1945

In the month of August 1940, the Orvietos (a well-known, established, and successful Jewish family from Rome) was on summer vacation in Magliano dei Marsi, in the Abruzzo region, about 50 miles east of Rome. The members of the Orvieto family were Enrico and Giuditta (Henry and Judith), Giuditta's mother, and their children: Gualtiero, Giuliano and Nathan.

Don Gaetano Tantalo, the pastor of St. Peter's church in Tagliacozzo about 3 miles away, happened to be in the same town for the funeral of one of his priest friends. He heard about the Jewish family and the deep dedication of their three children to the duties of their Jewish faith, and desired to visit them. That meeting established a solid friendship and a bond of mutual understanding and respect for each other's commitment to their religion.

In September of 1943, three years later, the German

army took over the Italian soil and started the persecution of the Jewish people and their shipment to the concentration camps up north.

Unfortunately, someone in Rome told the Germans about the Orvietos, but somehow the family made it out just in time to hide in their Magliano dei Marsi summer home. While there, they found out that their huge business warehouse had been destroyed completely. Soon the Germans were looking for them, so they moved to the nearby village of Poggio Filippo.

Around this time, for unknown reasons, a local farmer killed a German soldier which made it unsafe for the Orvieto family to stay there. Now they remembered Don Gaetano and thought of going to see him and asking him for his advice.

When Don Gaetano saw them, he said, "This is your house. God sent you here and here you will stay." From that day on, the Orvieto family moved into the small pastor's house and Don Gaetano took up residence with his sister Cucuccia's family, close by.

During the next nine months, Don Gaetano and the Orvieto family experienced a very close friendship based mostly on their mutual respect for each other's religious practices. Don Gaetano felt bad about his friends' present situation and tried to please them any way he could.

He deepened his knowledge of the Hebrew language so he could participate in the study of the Bible and for the coming celebration of Easter 1944. He was able to establish the exact date for Passover that year, Nisan 14, and for the occasion he found a new baking pan to make the pane azzimo, or matzo. Every single day, after spending many hours praying in church, he went up to the little house. Then, for at least an hour, he read and meditated on the sacred texts of the Bible.

Giuditta's brother, Pacifici, was a well-known rabbi in Genova, in North Italy, and around this time the Germans had taken him away to Germany. His destination was unknown.

After the front moved to the north, the Orvieto family took good care of the now very sick priest, Don Gaetano, scheduling appointments with the best doctors in Rome, but he died in 1947. They never forgot Don Gaetano, for whom they pledged to the authorities in Israel to dedicate a tree at the Yad Vashem, The World Holocaust Remembrance Center there. He is also remembered at the United States Holocaust Museum in Washington, D.C.

In 1956 his name was remembered at the Campidoglio in Rome, the headquarters of the Italian government and in 1982 a beautiful ceremony took place at the Yad Vashem in Israel.

To this day, the next generations of the Orvieto family continue their dedication to the process of canonization for their unforgettable friend, Don Gaetano.

OTHER REFERENCES

Pascucci, Tullio. *Don Gaetano Ci Guida Ancora: Gaetano Tantalo, Il Santo della Marsica Giusto tra i Giusti.* Avezzano, Italy: Edizioni Kirke, Ottobre 2017. 45+.

Tarquinio, Gianluca. *Musica e Musicisti a Tagliacozzo e Frazioni.* Avezzano, Italy: Edizioni Kirke. Dicembre 2017. 104+.